MODELLING
& ACTING FOR
KIDS

MODELLING & ACTING FOR

KIDS

From babies to teens –
a step by step guide to success

JANICE HALLY

A & C BLACK

First published 2004
A & C Black Publishers Limited
37 Soho Square, London W1D 3QZ
www.acblack.com

© 2004 Janice Hally

ISBN 0-7136-6797-4

A CIP catalogue record for this book is available from the British Library.

A & C Black uses paper produced with elemental chlorine-free pulp,
harvested from managed sustainable forests.

Typeset in 12 on 15pt ScalaSans

Printed and bound in Great Britain by
Biddles Ltd, King's Lynn

CONTENTS

ACKNOWLEDGEMENTS

I would like to acknowledge the valuable insights into the world of children's modelling and acting which I received from the many people who helped me with my research for this book.

Above all, I'd like to thank Janis and Stephen Penn and their son Simon for their time and help, and the unlimited access they allowed me to their agency *Scallywags* (www.scallywags.co.uk).

Thanks are due also to the professionals who spoke about the business from their particular perspectives, photographer Daniel Pangbourne (www.danielpangbourne.com), baby wrangler, Cat Sulley; casting director, Suzy Korel; television drama directors, Fiona Cumming and David Dunn; television producers, Peter May and Martyn Day; theatre director and writer, Charles Moritz; opera and theatre director, Robert Jones; and journalist Gavin Docherty.

For sharing their personal memories and their experiences, my thanks to former child models, David and Rachel York, and to former child actress, Evelyn Coull; also to Lesley Simpson, mother of model Tiffany, and Donna Hearn mother of models Rebecca and Charlotte.

And finally, a special thanks to The Bell Family, for the variety of viewpoints and relationships they encompassed: actor and singer Aidan Bell (www.aidanbell.com), his mother Hazel (www.aidanbell.com/html/hkbell.htm) and sister Diana, once a children's chaperone and now professional singer, Jezebel (www.aidanbell.com/html/sister.htm).

INTRODUCTION

This step-by-step guide is for child models, actors, young performers of every kind and the parents who will guide and look after them. If you want to break into the world of child modelling and acting, then this book will take you chapter-by-chapter through the process of assessing your child's suitability, finding an agent, and making a success of auditions and castings. When it comes to getting that first all-important job, there are explanations about what to expect on your first day at a film set or photographer's studio. You will learn about the etiquette of the workplace and will find out how to behave and what is expected of you. Knowing how to fit in as another member of the team will ensure that your child will get a good professional reputation and will be offered even more work. In addition, there are practical tips on looking after your child's earnings and keeping accounts, along with advice on dealing with life when your child's modelling or acting career comes to an end. There is also an important section on scams, how to spot them and how to avoid being taken in by the fraudsters who prey on vulnerable children and their parents.

There is no doubt that the jobs are out there. The demand for children is high. Top children's photographer Daniel Pangbourne confirms this, 'So many people want to use children in shots now – it's an enormous market.' And as each year's successful young models become a year older and move on, so the vacancies open up for new faces.

Drama on television and in movies includes many parts, large and small, for children. The advertising industry, with posters on hoardings, television commercials, and magazines, regularly features advertisements for food, toys, clothes, even cars, using babies and children. Modelling opportunities come in many different forms: sales catalogues, knitting patterns and on the packaging of products, too. Every day, all over the world, children are posing, performing and earning money – very often, a lot of money.

A point to consider

Before you find out how easy it can be, you should also know it can be a rocky road. You will encounter criticism – much of it based on genuine concerns. Some people are against the principle of children working as actors and models, claiming that it robs them of their childhood or their innocence. Others will assert that it can cause psychological problems for the children. Many people argue, with justification, that there are dangers involved and that you may fall prey to scams or paedophiles.

This guide will set out to provide you with sufficient information to protect yourself and your child from the hazards, perils and pitfalls of the business.

Being well-informed is the first step towards launching a safe and successful career for your child.

The second step is to ask yourself if it's really the right thing for you and your child to pursue. If you have a child who is pestering you to let them be involved in modelling or acting, then go straight to Chapter One. But if you have a child who is too young to understand what they are going to be involved in, then take some time to read the rest of this introduction.

A special note for parents of babies and toddlers

A baby or toddler can't express their opinion, so if you are a mother who is thinking of putting a very young child forward for modelling work then take a moment here to think about your reasons. You should never force your child into something for your own benefit or to pursue your own ambitions. Your child may get offered a lot of work and have the chance to make a lot of money, but if he or she can't do the job then it will lead to disappointment. Remember that it *is* a job. Further chapters will go on to describe the commitments and sacrifices you will have to make, but it will only be worthwhile if your child is happy doing it.

If your child doesn't have the right temperament or gets upset being around lots of different places and people, this will cause embarrassment and stress for you, and problems for the child. Above all, if your child isn't suited to the work, then you will go to interviews with agents and casting directors in vain.

On the other hand, if your baby or toddler isn't worried by strange, new environments, is bright, alert and curious, happy and content to be handled by strangers, enjoys attention and is easily encouraged to play games, then there is a good chance that they will have great fun getting out and about, going to auditions and photo shoots. Photographer Daniel Pangbourne says when people think of the modelling industry they may have images of pouting supermodels, he stresses, 'The kids' industry is a very different, soft industry. Really. It's good fun. It's full of very nice people who know how to deal with kids and babies. I know exactly how to get what a client wants from a child. The child doesn't know what they're doing in essence. You've got to know how to encourage it out. They just do what comes naturally, get treated very well, and have a good time. I think they get a lot out of it. It's a fun thing.'

Modelling or acting might also be something that they continue doing as they get older. It could end up paying for their university or college education, or might even provide them with a deposit on their first house. It could help their self-confidence, give them opportunities to travel, leave them with extraordinary memories and experiences and at the very least provide them with a unique photo album and record of their childhood.

If you think your child will be happy in the business and you decide to go ahead, then the next step is to read on.

You Must Have Been A Beautiful Baby
Types of jobs, and the qualities required to get them

Have you looked at children in television commercials or advertisements in magazines and thought, 'My child could do that. What makes these babies so special?' Perhaps you've heard about the large sums of money that advertisers are willing to pay to babies and small children. Easy money, it seems, when all the child has to do is to allow themselves to be filmed or to have a few pictures taken.

Those of you who are parents of babies and toddlers may have been prompted by friends and relatives to try to get your child into advertising. Perhaps you've had the experience of complete strangers stopping to tell you how beautiful your child is. It's a common experience for many people who have put their children forward for modelling. Donna Hearn, whose daughters Charlotte and Rebecca have been modelling for four years, says, 'It all started because people used to stop me in the street and say, "You know, your children are gorgeous. They've both got beautiful eyes. They should be models."'

Is being a beautiful baby all that it takes?
All sorts of children are in demand for acting and modelling work: any shape and size, from every ethnic background. Every agency will tell you how important it is for them to have the widest possible range of children on their books. Unlike adult modelling, where changing fashion dictates the 'beauty' of the moment, the sort of work available for children is much less glamourous and more down-to-earth. A company might want an adorable, big-eyed baby to add charm to their advertisement, but most of the advertising work involving children portrays them as part of an average family. For that reason your child doesn't have to be conventionally attractive; in fact, if they have the look of the 'child-next-door' they might

get most work of all. There is also a demand for quirky or unusual looking children – there can be a demand for 'characters' at the earliest of ages. In other words, there is the potential for work out there for all physical types and looks, with no hard and fast rules. Simon Penn, of top UK child modelling and acting agency Scallywags, says, 'It's hard to rule anyone out. You need the quirky kids, the funny kids, you can't have too many of just one style. It's possible to have too many really good-looking kids.'

What qualities does a child require?

A child has to *want* to be involved. Their desire to do the job is vital. From the first interview with an agent, through auditions, to keeping alert after a long day on a television set, if a child doesn't really want to do it, everyone will know it, and the child will simply not be employable or employed.

The child who will be be asked for, over and over again, is the child who is attentive and well-behaved; out-going and confident; interested in what they are doing. In other words, the child who *wants* to be there. Rachel York, a child model, now grown up and working for an agency, says, 'If a kid doesn't want to do it – even the tiniest baby – they will let you know about it. And if the kid doesn't want to do it, it's never going to work. No amount of pushing from the mother is going to make them do it.'

Perhaps you're the parent of an older child who has been bitten by the show business bug: singing and performing at the drop of a hat for strangers, taking dancing classes, or regularly landing the lead roles in school plays or musicals. Hazel Bell, mother of professional actor and singer Aidan Bell, says of her son, 'At the age of 11 he commandeered our garage, hanging curtains, selling cloakroom tickets for pennies through a backless tool cupboard, and assembling local children in rows to watch the shows in "The X Theatre", described in a handbill as "a small but life-size theatre". The programme boasted, "1 Whole hour of Immense Enjoyment ... Please come, youl (sic) love it!", but warned, "Children over 10 will not like it", and, "All children under 4 must be accompanied by a responsible person. Aidan has the right to turn out any hooligans and missbehaving (sic) persons!"' It's almost 30 years since Aidan wrote his own advertising handbills and took over the family garage. He has spent his whole life performing in the theatre and carving out a successful career in show business as a singer and actor.

My child doesn't just *want* to do it, my child wants to be a star!

A word of caution at this point to parents of 'star-struck' youngsters. Children are always eager to gain approval and if they sense that it is your dream for them to be on television or in films then they might go along with that to please you. If it is more *your* dream than theirs, agents and casting directors will quickly realise this. As you will discover later in the book, parents are as much under scrutiny during the interview and audition process as their children and nothing puts off an agent or casting director more than a pushy or star-struck parent. So make sure that it is your child who wants success and not just you.

Assuming that it is your child's dream, then talent and ambition are a great help, but it takes more than talent and ambition to succeed. The quality that makes a child star is impossible to define. It could be argued that the main factor involved is 'being in the right place at the right time'. If your ultimate aim is stardom, the way to begin is to learn the business. Getting regular work and succeeding in the world of child modelling and acting increase your chances of being seen, and being seen must greatly increase your chance of 'being in the right place at the right time'.

What are the modelling and acting jobs available for children?

Photographic work

This involves working on a shoot in a studio or on location with a photographer who will take pictures eventually destined to be used in advertisements for all sorts of products such as food and drink, toys, clothes, or cars and furniture. Photographs of child models also appear in sales catalogues and packaging, as well as in information or instructional material which accompanies products.

Newspaper and magazine PR work

To make a story look more appealing, newspapers and magazines sometimes set up photographs to accompany an article. The work involved would be similar to modelling on a photographic shoot.

Television or film drama

Series and serials or one-off films are made by national or independent production companies and are shot on location or in studio anywhere. Work on a drama production falls into two categories: 'featured roles' and 'extra work'.

Featured roles

Children can be cast in leading or starring parts. This will involve having to learn lines to speak and actions to perform.

Extra work

Children (or adults) who appear in the background of the story, in a crowd scene or simply walking through a scene with no lines to say and no name for their character, are extras. Someone who has to do something specific, with a line or two to deliver, is called a walk-on.

Television commercials

Children may have featured roles or be employed as extras in commercials. Commercials are made by independent production companies and are shot either in studio or on location anywhere. The crews are similar to those in drama productions, but the length of the shoot will be much shorter.

Documentaries

Sometimes television documentaries require real-life situations to be recreated. Recording or filming these scenarios will be very similar to television drama.

Television PR work

Daytime chat shows often require children to appear on the programme to animate a feature they are covering, such as dressing up in fancy dress for a feature on Hallowe'en, or appearing in a nativity scene at Christmas time. Sometimes the programme might have an item about children's clothing and require children to model the clothes, or an item about toys or gadgets and they require children to try the products out.

Television presenting
Children's television programmes sometimes have opportunities for children to work as presenters or news reporters for children's news programmes.

Stage performance
Children can find leading roles and extra or chorus work in theatre in dramas, musicals, operas, at any time of the year, but especially in pantomimes at Christmas time.

Solo performers
Some children may have a unique talent such as singing or playing a musical instrument and may find fame and fortune by performing in public.

What do professionals who are casting children look for when they first meet a child?
Agent, Janis Penn of top UK agency Scallywags, says, 'Eye contact. Am I going to get a performance out of this child if they can't even look at me? Through the eyes, intelligence and temperament show through. They can't hide their talent. We chat, and if I see potential there while I'm talking to them, I teach them how to give eye contact. I say, "Look here, at a spot at the top of my nose." I try to make them laugh, I tell them, "No you won't look cross-eyed! But when you go into an audition to see somebody, you have to look at their face. If you don't, they'll think you're too shy to do the job. If you want to do it, you're going have to convince them you can. So you have to learn to look at them right here." And in ten minutes you've taught them to make eye contact. It's easy. All the mums can teach their children to do this.'

Casting director, Suzy Korel says, 'Confidence ... and I check they're not just there because they have to be. I want to see whether or not they enjoy it. What pleases me is when it's *one* parent, *one* child, and the child walks in smiling, happy.'

Photographer, Daniel Pangbourne, who specialises in children's work, says, 'Babies, you can't ask much of. In the older ones ... confidence. Being able to speak to an adult, not hanging on to their mum's trouser leg and refusing to stand up. When I was a kid, I wouldn't have let go of my mum in a million years, but some kids are just great at it. They walk in and say, "Hello," as opposed to hiding and not being able to look at you. Just being able to say "Thank you" to you at the end of the day, makes a massive impression.'

Television director, Fiona Cumming says, 'I need to see that they're good at paying attention and listening. They have to be alert and easy to direct. Self-assured, but not too precocious.'

Writer and television producer, Peter May says, 'I look for the light in the eyes that says, "I can play this game! I want do this! Give me the part!". But it has to be natural. A theatrical performance is no good, it looks fake through the lens of a television camera. If a child is going to play a part convincingly, it has to come from inside. They have either got that ability or they haven't. And you can tell very quickly. If they have the ability to sit and talk confidently, intelligently and articulately at whatever age, you know you'll be able to get some kind of performance out of them. If a child can't meet your eye and sits staring downwards and scuffing their feet on the floor, they'll never be any good on television.'

Charles Moritz, over a number of years, wrote and directed for the Manchester Youth Theatre, and as part of that process, auditioned potential newcomers (in their mid-teens) for the company. He says, 'What we looked for in potential actors was energy, presence, interest and an unaffected approach to the whole business of theatre. If a youngster has potential and really wants to act then a youth theatre can be a fantastic training ground. It's best to arrive there as raw talent rather than carefully groomed.'

Special requirements

Before encouraging your child into the business, it is important that you examine the qualities required. You can see from the professionals' answers that they vary greatly depending on the type of job and the age of the child. The abilities demanded of a six month-old baby in a nappy commercial are quite different from the talents which producers will be looking for in a 16 year-old television actor. The following guide is divided into the different age groups and different jobs.

Babies and toddlers

First of all, remember that it's not always easy getting around town with a baby or toddler and all the paraphernalia they require. If it causes stress for you, that stress will quickly transfer itself to your child. You not only have to be sure that you will be able to cope with it, but you must also be sure that your young one can cope with it too. They have to be prepared for a lot of travelling to castings and jobs, and they must remain unaffected by it. When you arrive at an appointment, you will have very little time to settle and relax before being called to work.

As well as being able to settle quickly, your child will have to get used to being in strange locations. They will find themselves in lots of different places and unusual surroundings. Studios will be full of unfamiliar things; filled with strange noises and lights. Babies and toddlers will have to be happy in the company of people they don't know. If a film crew is involved, a very large number of people will be doing their jobs on set. Lots of faces the child doesn't recognise will be moving around them and interacting with them. This can be very frightening for a child who is only used to close family and friends.

They will have to be content to allow themselves to be handled by strangers. A model or actor might be playing 'mummy' to your child, or a 'baby wrangler' or assistant to the photographer or director might have to take them on to the set, to try to encourage them to make certain moves on camera. These people are professionals and used to handling children, therefore they will take great care of them, but if your child is not happy about being handled by someone they don't know, if they have a tendency to cling to you or suffer anxiety if you disappear from view, then they will not be suitable for this sort of work.

Naturally, babies and toddlers can tire easily – and you will be around to make sure that they are not over-worked – but in general they must have bright, alert demeanours, with a long attention span. You will know if they have a natural curiosity about new, exciting things, and if they are good at *paying* attention as well as *enjoying* attention.

The child who is well suited to this sort of work is one who enjoys playing, is responsive and can easily be encouraged to play games. An ability to mimic or respond to directions is one of the most useful qualities a tiny child performer can have.

Photographic, newspaper and magazine PR work

Photographers are looking for children who are self-confident, who have enthusiasm and energy but are able to focus and concentrate when required. They should be able to listen and follow simple instructions and, above all, should be well-behaved.

Television or film drama, television commercials, documentaries – featured roles

Being *considered* for a part will depend on being the right age, having the right look, and being able to behave naturally in front of cameras.

Winning the part will depend on making a special connection with the director or casting director.

What will be demanded later, after winning the part, includes the ability to learn lines, take direction and remember the timing of cues and actions, much of which will come with practice. It's also tiring work, demanding a great deal of concentration and the ability to keep focused. Shooting a drama can involve long hours of inactivity between being called on set to perform scenes. All actors, young and old, require patience and an ability to occupy themselves. It's important to be alert and ready to perform the minute you are called on set.

Television or film drama, television commercials, documentaries – extra work

It is much easier to get work as an extra than to win a featured role. Castings may be done by photographs alone, or by the production company giving an agent the specifications and leaving the agent to send along the children who are the right age and have the right look. Working as an extra can be an excellent way to gain experience and learn all about the workings of a television or a film shoot. An essential quality for every extra is patience. Being an extra involves a lot of waiting around to be called. Children must be well-behaved, able to keep themselves quietly occupied without getting bored but capable of switching their energy back on when called.

Television PR work

Directors will be looking for a confident child who won't be overwhelmed by the alien environment of a television studio. Its bright lights can be dazzling and hot. Large cameras gliding across the floor, tilting and flashing can be very frightening for a small child. The child must have a good personality and be happy and natural, as well as gregarious and able to chat to anybody. Spontaneous interviews can form a part of this kind of work, so the ability to speak confidently and to speak up clearly is an advantage.

Television presenting

Everything mentioned above applies, but additionally, because presenting is more structured and will involve older teenagers, the demands are greater. A presenter must have self-confidence; the ability not only to follow a script, but to be able to be spontaneous for interviews. When casting a presenter, producers will be looking not just for a sparkling and appealing personality, but also for a quick wit and clever mind. Many programmes with presenters are done live, in studio, therefore a lot of responsibility rests on the shoulders of a presenter. As the comedy programmes which feature out-takes demonstrate, things can often go wrong, and when they do, it is the person on screen who takes the brunt of it. Being able to improvise is essential.

Stage performance

There are a limited number of opportunities, but for stage work, a child might be called upon to have specific talents, such as the ability to sing or dance or both. Often, recruitment for theatre shows will be done through local choirs or dance schools. Occasionally there will be an advertisement for an open audition. At open auditions, a child will have a matter of minutes to show off their skills before the casting director will move on to the next child. With so little time, the child who wins through to get a part in the show is the child who can produce the goods on demand and knock out the casting director. Only the most extrovert and confident children are suited to a career on the stage.

Solo performance

As with the children who are drawn to the stage, the child who is suited to solo performance must be an extrovert. They will have a unique talent, often musical, and will love to demonstrate it to friends, family and anyone else who will listen. As well as talent, they will have dreams and ambitions.

To make a career as a solo performer requires the most self-assured child of all. Their biggest problem is not in attracting the attention of a director or casting director, but in finding the correct vehicle to show themselves off. Often it can come through finding parts in theatre or television which feature their talent. Sometimes it can come through entering talent competitions. In many cases, children with unique abilities create their own opportunities. If parents of a child with a special talent want to encourage their child in their dreams of a career in show business, then all they can do is support their child and grasp opportunities wherever they arise. Children like this are the most determined of all. The road certainly won't be easy and they'll need the support, encouragement and understanding of their parents.

What are the qualities a parent requires?

Of course, as a parent, you believe that your child is the most beautiful or talented child in the world. You probably love the idea of seeing your child on television. You would be proud to show friends and relatives professionally-taken photographs or your child in advertisements or catalogues. But every parent embarking on a career in modelling or acting for their child must be sure that they have their child's best interests at the forefront of their mind.

Are you star-struck?

You may think that the world of modelling, show business, television and film is exotic and exciting and that entering that environment will allow you to rub shoulders with the rich and famous. Perhaps you believe that being involved in it will provide a passport to a more glamourous life for your child and yourself. But if these are your priorities, then you are almost guaranteeing that your child will not be successful. No one wants to work with a star-struck mother or father.

Are you a frustrated performer yourself?

Perhaps you always loved performing and wish that as a child you could have appeared on stage or television. Your child may well have opportunities that you never had. You may feel that they're very lucky and shouldn't pass up the chance, if they get it, to break into the business. But beware of using your child to live out your dreams. Ask yourself if it is *really* what your child wants.

It's possible that your children do share your enthusiasm and talent for performing. In the case of Hazel Bell's family, it seems that acting was in the blood, she explains, 'My mother, Kay Macaulife, Aidan's grandmother, was a professional actress. She was a member of Bognor Repertory Company. Until I was 16, I attended dancing classes that put on frequent concerts and an annual pantomime, as well as appearing whenever a child was wanted in the many productions my mother was involved in with the Women's Institute, Falcheham Players and the Repertory Theatre. My mother told me, after the (non-) event, that the producer of Bognor Rep Company had wanted to put on "Children in Uniform" with me in the lead. My mother refused permission (and didn't tell me), on the grounds that it would interfere with my school work. I bitterly resented that when I learned it – in fact, still do, when I think of it! How I would have *loved* to have played the lead for a week at Bognor Rep! So – I have *never* denied such a chance to Aidan. Let children set their own priorities for their time, energies, enjoyment – as feasible.'

Hazel's son, Aidan Bell agrees that performing was in his blood, 'I think that I would not separate my ambition into "childhood' and 'adult" periods. Other than the obvious maturity that comes with adulthood, I think my "dream" has remained throughout my life. All that adulthood does is to allow the (supposed) wisdom of years to shape how one approaches one's dreams and I'm certainly one of those adults who hopes that they will never grow up anyway! I think I was born with a genetic, inbuilt desire that led me inevitably into showbusiness. It's in my blood and I think it's as natural to me as having two arms and breathing.'

Are you motivated by the money that your child could earn?

It is true that some children make a great deal of money, especially those who are in demand for television commercials. If a child enjoys acting or is happy posing for pictures, then their earnings can seem to come as very easy money indeed. It's obvious that there are many advantages to be gained from the extra cash. Perhaps the money is one of the reasons that you are looking into the subject? Perhaps you are thinking that if it's something your child could easily do, then why not, what's the harm? But if money is the motivation for you encouraging your child to work, then you might be tempted to put pressure on your child to do it. Money must never take precedence over your child's welfare and no parent should put pressure on a child to go into the business of modelling or acting.

As a parent, your child's interests and well-being must always come first

Never lose sight of the fact that the child must *want* to do it: casting directors or producers will be quick to notice if that's not the case. Also remember that your attitude is vitally important. If you are a pushy parent you will put professionals off. If your child really wants to go into the business, what they need from you is encouragement and support, and the knowledge that they are safe, that you are there protecting them and looking after their interests.

CHAPTER ONE CHECKLIST

A child model or actor must:
- have a strong desire to do the work
- be involved and interested in the work
- be attentive and well-behaved
- be confident and outgoing
- have a good memory for repeating lines or actions
- have good levels of stamina and concentration

Babies and toddlers must:
- be unaffected by travelling to castings and jobs
- be able to settle quickly in different places with strange noises and lights
- be happy in the company of people they don't know (sometimes a large number of people if a film crew is involved)
- be content to allow themselves to be handled by strangers
- not cling to parents or suffer anxiety if parents disappear from view
- be bright and alert
- be curious and attentive
- have a long attention span
- enjoy attention
- be responsive and easily encouraged to play games
- be able to mimic or take direction

Important Dos and Don'ts for parents
Parents must never:
- be motivated by wanting simply to 'show off' their child on television or in magazines
- be 'star-struck', wanting to break into what is perceived as a glamorous environment
- live out their own unfulfilled dreams of performing through their child
- be motivated by money and the expectation of making an easy fortune

Parents must always:
- put the child's best interests first
- be sure that the child really *wants* to do it
- be supportive
- be encouraging
- be protective

Remember that your child's well-being must be your first priority.

CHAPTER TWO
Don't Put Your Daughter on the Stage, Mrs Worthington
Other issues to consider before entering the business

You've now taken a long, hard look at your child and you've decided that your child has all the qualities necessary for acting or modelling. You're sure that they really want to do it, or in the case of the very young ones, you're sure that they will be suited to it and will enjoy the experience.

The next step is to take some time to consider the effect that this will have, not only on your child's life, but on your own. The effects can be both positive and negative, but above all, you must realise that things will never be the same again.

For most children, getting a modelling or acting job means having a fun day out. In addition, they'll be earning money, gaining experience of life, travelling, meeting people and building up self-confidence. But before you take the decision to go ahead you should be aware of the pressures involved too. The whole family will have to adapt and make changes to accommodate a young performer in the household. To leap into the business of putting your child forward for modelling and acting work without weighing all of this up is a very dangerous move.

What are the side-effects of modelling or acting on a child and their family?
Broadening horizons
Going out to castings, auditions and jobs gets both you and your child out of the house. You may get the chance to travel to interesting locations. You will meet lots of new people and you'll get the opportunity to do and see things which are away from your usual routine. This can have positive side-effects for both you and your child. Lesley Simpson speaks of her personal experience, 'I had been ill and my friend was worried about the fact that

Tiffany and I were not getting out enough. My friend had just joined Scallywags and she suggested it really as a way for me to be getting out and about. That's how it started. My friend even drove me to the audition.' Although apprehensive at first, Lesley found that it had a beneficial effect on both her and Tiffany. Tiffany has enjoyed the work so much that she wants to become a professional dancer when she gets older.

Discipline and patience

You and your child will have to be disciplined and be able to deal with pressure and boredom. Getting a job, means just that. You will be going to work with other professionals who are working hard and keeping to strict schedules. When you commit yourself to a job, you are also committing yourself to a level of professionalism. Working in television or film can mean getting up and being on the road very early to meet a wardrobe and make-up call. Once you are there, you have to be prepared for long hours of doing nothing while you wait to be called. You have to realise and accept from the start that this is how it will be. It can be very trying, and there is no alternative but to learn to be patient.

Self-confidence and maturity

The rewards for a child model or actor can be increased self-confidence and maturity. If your child has a talent for it, if you treat the job as a day out, it can be a fulfilling experience with benefits for the youngsters involved. Donna Hearn is unequivocal when she describes her daughters' reaction to working, 'They *love* it!'. For a child who enjoys it, there are many things to be gained. Donna explains that her girls have grown up with modelling being very much a part of their lives. They don't think there's anything unusual about working. In answer to the question of whether working has changed them in any way, Donna can only think of positive effects, 'It's given them so much confidence at school. Charlotte especially. She had to get up and read in front of the whole school recently and when she did it, she got a huge round of applause. There are a couple of other girls in her class who are just as clever, but they lack the confidence to be able to do that.'

Lesley Simpson, whose daughter Tiffany is a model, agrees. She feels that her daughter has more poise and self-assurance, 'Even the teachers say it. Her teacher last year said, "Tiffany is very versatile. She can have a conversation with the other children and then she can turn to the adults and have a conversation with them, but not as a child. She's speaking to the adults on their level."' Lesley feels that this comes from working in an adult environment, where the professionals around Tiffany are doing their jobs and treating Tiffany just as they would another professional in the workplace.

David York, a very successful child model and actor, now grown up, also feels that working with adults was beneficial to him, 'Obviously being a child, in an adult environment, they give you a little bit more space, they make sure you're well-treated, look after your welfare. But at the same time, you're out there working on a lot of jobs, and you're learning how the world works.' He never felt that his education suffered. He says, 'On the contrary. I learned a lot more when I was working. I was doing and seeing things I'd never otherwise get the opportunity to do in school. I was being prepared for life. I was learning communication skills, dealing with people. I was out there in the real world. And you learn that, okay, this place is really big, but around you people are just people, doing jobs. You're definitely better equipped to cope with life!'

Rachel York, David's sister, who is also a former child model, agrees, 'I think it matured me. You have to interact with adults in a way that you normally don't get the chance to as a kid. You get to know the way to behave.'

Photographer, Daniel Pangbourne sees the effect on children he works with, 'It's great fun for the kids to mix with adults, working in an adult environment. Apart from the fact that they get money and it's a nice day out, and they get treated well ... the confidence the kids build from it is amazing.'

Some will claim that mixing in an adult environment causes the child to grow up too quickly and that they miss out on normal childhood. Hazel Bell's response is, 'What I always feel on hearing this, is ... what's so marvellous about a so-called "normal" childhood? It seems often to consist of hanging about the streets, boredom, fighting, bullying or being bullied! What could possibly be nicer than spending your childhood doing just what you most enjoy?'

Stresses and pressures

There is also the possibility of a child having to cope with adult stress and pressure at work. The world of modelling and acting is full of professionals trying to do a job and keep to budgets and schedules. It can be a stressful environment. Television and film crews, as well as photographers, are working in a business where time is money. If people make mistakes and things begin to take longer than they should, then the pressure will begin to grow. A child will sense this pressure around them, and it will take a strong personality and a level head to be able to perform and get their performance right under these conditions.

Problems with school work

There can be problems at school. Missing school might cause a child to fall behind and not keep on top of school work. A child who enjoys modelling and acting will be less likely to admit that they are having problems at school. Their priority is likely to be that they would prefer to do the thing they enjoy the most. What child would choose maths revision rather than a day out filming a television commercial with their football-star hero? But many youngsters actually do better rather than worse at school because they are well motivated and confident as a result of their experience working. For those who might be vulnerable, protection exists in legislation which strictly limits the number of days that a child can miss school in any six-month period. Children working on longer projects such as a movie, must, by law, have a tutor provided by the production company. Nevertheless, it will be important for parent and child not to let the novelty and excitement of working take precedence over getting a fully-rounded education. Parents should pay special attention and look out for any signs of slipping grades.

Resentment from other children

Other children at school can make life difficult for a child who is acting or modelling. Simply seeing their schoolmate on television might motivate children to drive home the point that they think he or she is nothing special and they can have cruel and uncompromising means of doing so. They might also be envious of the money a child model or actor earns. The most modest child might be accused of acquiring airs.

Even trying to keep the work secret, doesn't always work, as David York recalls, 'There can be lots of problems arising from jealousy. My mum always told me not to talk too much about what I did. It made me very self-deprecating. I always used to try to play it down. I'd say to my friends that yeah, I was doing stuff for TV or whatever, but that I was rubbish really. I did get bullied a little bit at school. It wasn't just because of the modelling – but I reckon that it might have been a factor. It makes you a bit more aware. You're doing this great stuff. You know inside you're good. You're happy with it. But you know that you just can't say too much about it because the other kids don't appreciate it.'

Hazel Bell recalls her son Aidan's time at school, 'Entering the school full of enthusiasm and curiosity, he suffered bullying and the disruption of interesting lessons. I thought the school entirely irresponsible. When we complained of bullying to the form master, he said, "Tell the year master," who said, "Tell the head master." The general principle was children should learn to hit back. Not a good policy to advocate to pacifists, or for the good of society overall.' But Aidan's love of theatre proved to be a source of comfort, 'Aidan came to enjoy only the music and drama. The miserable school years were relieved by many school plays and drama classes, and playing percussion in orchestras.'

Disruptions to family life
You must make yourself available at any time, which can disrupt family life. Going to auditions is time-consuming. You will have to be flexible and able to rearrange things in your life around casting and jobs. You and your child may have to make sacrifices: having to cancel a family outing or football or swimming practice if a casting comes up at short notice. Rachel York, former model, now working in a child modelling agency says, 'We might call you and tell you we've got a job or a casting ... can you be

there tomorrow? Some mums drop everything – and that's great – you really do have to be flexible if you want to be a success.'

In some extreme cases, some people have cancelled the family holiday because a particularly good opportunity has come up for a child. While the work and the pay-cheque may be exciting for the child concerned, you can imagine the disappointment this could cause for other family members.

Getting the children to interviews, auditions and castings at the drop of a hat will sometimes also be at the expense of other children in the family. Often you will be called on at very short notice and will have to make arrangements quickly. If there are other young children in the family you may have to have child-minder on call. Hazel Bell talks about becoming a chauffeur for her son Aidan, 'Saturdays became taken up by driving him to weddings to sing and earn a few pence less than the cost of the petrol to get him there and back!' She recalls, 'I think the most boring was having to hang around at rehearsals etc. to wait to take Aidan home, the alternative being four drives, take him there, go home, later return to collect him. And, classes in St Albans, seven miles away, after school, were a nuisance.' But Hazel is philosophical about it, 'We had three children, all needing different chauffeuring! It comes with the territory if you have children. It was the same with our elder son, whose first part-time job was strawberry picking, some miles away. What would I have been doing instead? What would I put before servicing the children?'

Rivalry between siblings

There can be problems for other family members, in particular, between siblings, where rivalry is difficult to avoid in children too young to be objective. Rachel York, who is David's sister, remembers when she felt she had had enough of the work, 'I had the blond ringlets and the cute little face. Perfect for photographic work, but not for commercials. When they traipsed you round for jobs I got very fed up. Even now I'm not a very patient person – but then, I was so impatient. I would be sitting in castings, saying "When am I going to be seen? When am I going to be seen, so that we can go?" I didn't like doing castings. That's why I was quite happy to stop when I was 12. I mean I'd been doing it since I was three. But if a kid doesn't want to do it – you can't make them.' Rachel goes on to speak about the difficulties which can arise between siblings who are both in the modelling business, 'David, my brother, is probably the most patient person I've ever known. He was a very beautiful, bonny, cute little boy, and he got jobs and was out working *all* of the time. I was always asking "Why am I not working?" And my mum would say, "You don't want to do it – you had a casting and you said you didn't want to go." I still couldn't accept the fact that David was going for jobs and getting them, and meeting famous people. I didn't understand that I had to be like him to get ahead. I just thought ... "He's getting it, why can't I?" But we're very different. He's got an amazing level of patience, and an ability to get on with anyone. I'm not like that. He had all the big money coming in as well. I wouldn't say I was jealous – but I just didn't understand why he had it and I didn't. But he earned it. He was always working.'

With a child performer in the family there could be other effects on his or her brothers and sisters, which may be overlooked. Diana Bell, Aidan's sister says, 'I was so determined *not* to be compared to my brother, I decided to ignore my own desires to be a singer and went into two alternative careers.' Diana started working in childcare, but she was still drawn to the world of performance and theatre and was a chaperone for child actors before going on to become a West End theatre manager. Eventually she was able to fulfil her real ambition and now works professionally as a singer in Greece, under the name of Jezebel. 'I only started singing in my 20s, once Aidan had moved to Austria and was out of the picture. I now know that had I started much, much younger, I'd be far more successful than I turned out to be.'

Simon Penn of Scallywags agency has also encountered problems involving siblings. 'We've got a couple of sisters aged 15 and 16 on our books. The older one is very much in demand, but the younger one isn't getting so much work. We got a job offer recently for the older one and I called up to speak to her. Her mother answered the phone and was really interested to hear that it was the agency with a job, until she heard the job was for the older one. When we told her that, she started to back off saying, "Oh I'm not sure if she'll be able to make it." And without checking with her daughter to see whether she could or couldn't make it, she just told us we'd better just turn it down. We suspect it's because she's trying to balance things out for the girls. But that's a shame because work comes and goes. It might be one at the moment, but it could be the other one who will be getting all the work next year.'

Donna Hearn remembers a time when both of her daughters were put forward for a job in Spain, 'They were both shortlisted, and then the agent phoned and said "Get your passport ready – Charlotte's got it!" I was worried for Rebecca, worried about how she would take it. Rebecca's younger, she's just seven and Charlie's nine. Anyway, as it happened, 24 hours before we were due to go, it was cancelled. I was secretly quite relieved. I wasn't happy at the idea of competition between them. I don't like it when they're both going for the same job. I don't know if it would have bothered *them* that much – I'm sure they would have been pleased for one another – but it was *me*! I don't like the feel of it, if one is favoured over the other one.'

Any parent knows that even under normal circumstances competition between siblings is a risk. It's important to be sensitive to the dreams and ambitions of all the children in a family. If one child is particularly good at anything, their siblings can feel overshadowed. In the case of the child performer, however, this is more pronounced. They will draw attention and focus to themselves – inside and outside of the family – far more than a child with any other talent.

Criticism from other people
You will face criticism from other people. The attention which child performers attract is not always positive. Having a child who is getting jobs as an actor or a model can draw strong disapproval from outside of the immediate family. Friends, relatives, teachers and members of authority will express opinions and pass comment on your decision to let your child work.

Be prepared for some of the arguments you will hear:
■ children are being exploited when they are involved in the advertising or entertainment business
■ you are robbing your child of their childhood and innocence
■ you are using your child to make money
■ you are exposing them to a harsh working environment and putting them under stress and anxiety

People will cite the famous examples of Hollywood child stars who have gone off the rails and ended up dependent on drugs or even committing suicide.

Rachel York says, 'Some people throw their hands up in horror at the thought of children working and think, "Oh no! It's just like sending them ... up the chimneys ... down the coal mines!" The truth is, it's nothing like that at all. They're in a studio, sitting on a couch for the most of the day, then they get up and they do their bit. I was treated like a little princess. They'd come and ask if I wanted some sweets, or drinks, or toys ... anything I wanted.'

There are also restrictions on the amount of work a child can do. They can only work certain hours, or a fixed number of days within a six-month period, so Rachel feels the child is well protected, 'No kid is working so much that they can't go to their friend's house, or they can't go the park. So, I'd never say it robs someone of their childhood. Not at all.'

Photographer Daniel Pangbourne, agrees, 'Everyone's bound by laws and regulations designed to protect any child from being exploited. It's a situation where everybody wins: the child gets money, they get experience of working in an adult environment, they get the chance to do something fantastic, and the clients get the best image to convey their product, or book, or clothes. On top of all that, it's a really nice industry to be in. It really is. Much better than, say, the adult fashion industry or the adult model industry.'

When faced with criticism, in some cases you will be certain that the accusations do not apply to you or your own family situation and will be able to respond appropriately; on other occasions, people may be expressing fears and genuine concerns about real dangers. Later in the book you will learn how you can protect your child from the hazards inherent in the business.

Handling your accusers will require diplomacy on your part, which is why you must take the time before you start to consider your children's feelings and well-being, as well as your own motives for going ahead. As long as you are convinced that it is the right thing for you and your family, then you will be able to make a reasoned argument against those who criticise you. On other occasions, however, you might never hear their disapproval, you might only feel the effect of it.

David York talks about how people can be envious and disapprove of children earning large sums of money, but instead of expressing it, it manifests itself in unusual ways. 'Take the licensing situation ...' Children have to be licensed to work. This involves getting approval from their school and local authority. These licences are used to check that a child is not asked to work more than the maximum number of days which are legal in a six-month period, and that they are working for a bona fide company. David explains, 'There's a lot of paperwork involved, forms to fill in – you need birth certificates, doctor's letters, school letters, clearance from the local authorities. People think that you just turn up, get a few photographs taken and that's it, but there's a huge amount of hassle and paperwork involved that people don't know too much about. And at every stage you might encounter people who think, "Why are these kids getting the chance to make this sort of money?" And it's entirely possible that they might take the opportunity to make things difficult for you. Papers can get lost or held up, or permission denied.'

Financial issues

You must be prepared for the fact that your child could make large sums of money. It's hard to see a disadvantage to earning money. The benefits to your child will be tangible. It is important to remember that the money belongs to the child. It has to be paid into the child's account although you will retain control over it. Many people allow the children to spend just a little of it before investing the rest of it for their child's future. Other people allow their children to spend it as they wish. The experiences and advice from ex-models and parents of models will be found later in the book. You will have to decide what is best for your own family.

Running a business

You will be running a business and will have to take it seriously. A parent will receive a fee as a chaperone. You must remember that this fee is being given to you to do a job. It's your responsibility to get your children to work on time and to look after them in the workplace. You must make sure that you know the regulations governing the type of work your child is doing, and your child's rights. All agents will have the most up-to-date details.

You will also have to remember that a working child is, in effect, running a self-employed business. You will have to account for all the money your child earns as well as the expenses incurred. You will find more information and basic guidance on how to do this in Chapter Eight.

A final word from a mother who has been through it all ...

Donna Hearn, mother of model daughters, doesn't feel that there have been any serious side-effects for her family, 'We're just really normal. Obviously I'm *very* proud – I've got lovely pictures of them. I've got about 20 videos from all sorts of television work. Some of the commercials are really cool. I've got stunning pictures of them to look back on, really nice magazine shots and fun stuff too. I'm so proud. And although it's nice that they've got a little nest egg, I would have done it for nothing because to see your children like that – it's priceless.'

CHAPTER THREE
Let Me Entertain You
Taking the first steps to find work

If you've weighed up all the difficulties you may face, and you're still determined to go ahead, the next step is to decide whether to go it alone or to find an agent: the decision depends both on the ambitions of your child and the type of work they will be trying to get.

Is an agent really necessary?
Modelling
Modelling jobs for children are almost exclusively to be found through agents. Advertising agencies and casting directors are too busy to advertise and hold open castings for every single job. They will either look first in the model books (books which agencies produce containing photographs of all the models they represent) or they will go straight to an agent with a description of the type of children they need. From that description, the agencies will look through their models and draw up a list of children who fit the requirements. The casting director or photographer will then liaise with the agency to arrange times and locations for castings. It would be virtually impossible to find modelling work without having an agent. Exceptional circumstances might be if you spot an advertisement or a feature in a newspaper announcing an open competition run by a manufacturer who is searching for a newcomer to become the new 'face' of their product; but these opportunities will only occur very rarely and such competitions are usually nothing more than vehicles for free publicity and promotion for the company involved. For the thousands of children who enter, there is a chance of a contract for just one lucky child at the end of it. It's also worth bearing in mind that when a child becomes famous for being associated with one product it is then virtually impossible to get work with any other company.

Acting

Stage schools, local drama groups and youth theatres might provide useful contacts in the business. Open auditions may be advertised occasionally in newspapers for parts in films, television and theatre, but as with the competitions described previously, these are more often publicity stunts for a production, than a serious way to find work. It is possible that an unknown child will spot an advertisement in *The Stage*, and will go along to an open audition and land a major role in the next 'Harry Potter' film, but agents are invariably the first to find out about such auditions and will ensure that their clients get to meet the producer or director. Agents will also be the first stop for production companies who are hiring people for extra work in films and television. An agent will be told the number and type of children that the production company are looking for. If the agent is trusted and has a good relationship with the production company the children will be sent along to work on the day without an audition being required.

Stage or Musical performance

If your child has dreams of a career singing or playing an instrument, either solo or as part of a group, initially they will have to make their own opportunities. The methods include entering talent competitions, sending tapes or CDs of themselves to recording companies, and trying to secure bookings for themselves to perform live. There are, from time to time, advertisements in *The Stage* or music magazines for auditions to form a new boy band or girl band. You should never have to pay any money to audition (see *Scams*, in Chapter Four) and if your youngster wins through and is offered a contract make sure that you have it checked over by a lawyer before signing anything. They will have to try to promote themselves by convincing people to book them to perform, perhaps at weddings, private parties or clubs. Some agents might take on a child with a special talent, but they will normally want some evidence of success first. Training and rehearsing will be their main activity.

What are the advantages of having an agent?

There is no doubt that having an agent will help you to advance your child's modelling or acting career.

Agents have the necessary contacts

Agents are connected with all the professionals in the business. They have all the contacts with people who are providing the work. Casting directors, advertising agencies, producers, directors and photographers will only go to well-known modelling and acting agencies. An agent will be the first person to get notification about a job coming up and can be trusted to put a suitable child forward for auditions. On your own, as a member of the general public, you would never find out about these jobs.

Many agents produce a model book

The big agencies produce a model book which they send out to hundreds of clients. It includes photographs of all the children on their books, and ensures that their models are seen by literally *thousands* of professionals in the business. This is much more effective than sending out individual photographs which are overlooked, filed away and forgotten about or lost.

Agents vet and assess the children they take on

Casting directors, producers and photographers who are casting children are normally working to a tight schedule. They would never have time to advertise and invite applications for every part which comes up. Imagine how long it would take to sift through hundreds of different enquiries with photographs; then to decide on a short-list and make 20 or 30 telephone calls to individuals to try to make appointments and arrange to meet them for a casting. The task of finding the right child is made much easier if they simply go to an agent. They will then be sent a selection of children, already vetted for their ability and suitability, who meet their requirements in terms of looks, and who have already proved themselves capable of doing the work. Casting directors know that children coming through an agent will be professional and know what is involved and expected when they come to a job. This is especially true for extras in film or television drama or commercials as Janis Penn explains, 'For extra work, or featured extras, a company will ask us for various children, whom they choose from photographs in the book. But then, we have a good reputation. Most of the clients know that we're not going to send someone along who'll wreck the studio or not do the job. Our clients know us – they know we're going to send children who are going to perform for them.'

An agent is the mark of your professional attitude

If you want to work often, you will have to take the business seriously: this entails being professional. Being represented by an agent increases how professional you look.

An agent provides you with security

You have an element of protection against unscrupulous individuals if you are represented by an agent (see *Scams*, in Chapter Four). Agents will ensure that the jobs they send children out to do are professional and safe. Many of the casting directors or production companies are long-term clients of a model and acting agency.

Photographer Daniel Pangbourne says, 'All the shots I do are for reputable clients, and they're known to the agency. So when a child joins the agency, the child has the security of of knowing all that has been checked out, that they're not being ripped off and they're not entering a situation which is wrong for them or dangerous for them. They also know they're going to be paid. By going through the agency, the agency is guaranteeing that they get paid the proper fees for the job – so there isn't the chance of exploitation in that sense – they're being paid the proper rate for it – and under contract.'

An agent will also invoice the production company for payments on behalf of the child. Sometimes there can be long delays, but an agent is equipped to pursue companies for payments, enforcing court orders if necessary to ensure that the payment is made.

How do you find an agent?
Word of mouth
First, ask around to find out if anyone you know, knows anyone involved in the business. A personal recommendation is one of the best ways to be sure that you will be safe approaching an agency. If this draws a blank, you will have to do some research. But take care, there are a lot of frauds, scams, and potential dangers in the business, so follow the suggestions below, and go through a careful process of checking before you commit to anything.

Call up companies who use child model agencies
Look up the telephone numbers of advertising agencies, or catalogues or magazines who might use child models. Ask them which agencies they use and trust.

The Yellow Pages
Agencies which are used by people you know or by major companies should be at the top of your list to approach. But you can add to your list by checking out the Yellow Pages. Begin by searching under 'Child Model and Acting Agencies'. Some adult agencies also handle children but the amount of work that they regularly get for children can vary – so you will have to ask them some specific questions (see *Questions to ask an agency* later in this chapter) to find out whether or not they will be right for you. Information is limited in the Yellow Pages. Start by making an initial list of names, addresses and telephone numbers.

The Internet
If you have access to a computer and the Internet, check to see if any of these agencies have websites. An agent's website will have more information about their clients and their policies for accepting new models.

Be wary if you find an agency which has a website but does not appear to have an entry in the Yellow Pages. Remember that it is possible for anyone to set up a website. A presence on the Internet does not guarantee that a company is reputable. Read more about this in the section on *Scams* in Chapter Four.

Make initial contact by telephone

Once you have compiled a list of agencies, decide which ones you want to approach first. An initial phone call is worthwhile to find out if the agency is interested in looking at new children or if they have any special requirements.

One thing which is on your side at this stage is that children grow up very quickly. They are constantly changing and moving on, therefore most agencies who deal with children are usually on the look-out for new faces.

What will an agent ask you to provide?

When you phone and ascertain that an agency is interested in seeing more children, do not expect to be invited to the office straight away for an interview.

Photographs

In general, an agency will ask you to send in a photograph or two and some details. (**N.B.** This does not mean that your next step is to hurry out and pay for an expensive folio of photographs taken by a professional.) Janis Penn of Scallywags says, 'If a child's mother phones up and says "We have a folio" we tell her we don't want to see it. We ask to see the child in a snapshot because we need to know what they look like at their most natural.' All that an agent requires of a child is a family snapshot or individual school portrait, perhaps two or three, with at least one showing the child's face, and one showing full body. They should be in focus, clear, well-exposed photographs with no accessories obscuring your child.

Janis Penn says, 'They should send two recent snapshots. Full face, not with a hat on. Not with a baby all covered in ice cream, or bowl of spaghetti over the head. We've had all of that. Parents think it's cute. But what we need are nice, clear, recent snapshots which show the child's face. One head and shoulders shot, and one full length.'

You should write your child's name clearly on the back of the photographs, along with your own name and address, in case the photographs become separated from your letter.

Details about the child

Next, take a sheet of paper and write (or preferably, type) out the following details about you and your child:

Your name
Child's name
Address
Date of birth
Height
Clothing size
Hair colour
Eye colour

List their special talents, e.g. singing, dancing, sports and hobbies (advertisers may ask for a child who can skateboard, swim, or play football); and anything else which you think might be relevant. This is very important – any qualities which make your child special or unique may help them to get a job.

Put this sheet together with the photographs.

Finally, enclose a stamped envelope, addressed to yourself, large enough that the agency can use it to return your photographs and reply to you. It should not take long for the agency to write back with a decision.

What will the agent do next?

Every reputable agent should reply within a short space of time, telling you if they are interested in seeing your child, or not.

If you receive a rejection from an agent, it doesn't mean that your chances of getting into the business are over. It may simply be that your child doesn't have the right look at the moment. Different agents have different requirements. It might also be a matter of waiting a year or two, as Donna Hearn found out, 'When Charlotte was little I sent a photo off and the agent told me that they had enough people on their books at that time. Then I sent a photograph with the two girls together, when Rebecca was nearly a year old. Again I was told no, they weren't taking any more on at that time, but I should try again later. So, third time around, I tried and they both got accepted. They've been doing it for four years now, and every single year since they were accepted, they've done really well.'

Janis Penn says, 'We would write back, more or less straight away, telling applicants, either that we don't think they're suitable for us or, that we want to proceed to meet with the child. In which case, we send them a whole series of information sheets along with their photographs when we return them. We explain the whole process to them. The first step is that they would come in to see us for an assessment. They need to phone us for an appointment and there is a fee for this session, for our time, and because we have to set up a photographer and lighting. These initial photographs taken at the assessment are used by us in the first instance for reference. If they choose to join us then it means that we have good, professional-quality photographs to represent them with straight away. We can get them up on the computer records immediately. They don't then have to go and get a folio done which can be very expensive.'

All agencies are different, so make sure you ascertain if they intend to charge a fee, and if so, ask what the fee is for (see *Scams*, in Chapter Four).

A special note about family modelling

There are an increasing number of opportunities for families in modelling. Whenever a company requires a family for a photographic shoot or a television commercial, they have to take special care to match up the adults to the children so that they look as if they could be the real parents. Janis Penn says, 'In these cases we can use whole families. Instead of a company putting a family together they can just get a whole family from us.' One or both parents plus children – all the brothers and sisters – may be used in any combination or all together for a photographic or modelling job. If you think that you would like your family to be assessed for this sort of potential, mention this to the agent in advance.

How to present yourself and your child at an interview with an agent

If your snapshots appeal to the agent and they invite you to make an appointment for an interview or assessment, this is the first test for you and your child.

The first and most important point is that – unless you have been invited to bring more than one child to be assessed – it should *only* be you and the child concerned who make the trip to the agent. You have to be able to give your full attention to the interview. It is not acceptable to turn up at interviews with agents, or for jobs, with the entire family in tow. No agent wants to interview a mother and child if the mother is constantly distracted by trying to handle another three children or toddlers. If both parents want to attend this initial interview, then that is acceptable, but do remember that when you go to jobs, only one chaperone will be expected to attend with each child (you will find out more about this in the chapters dealing with auditions and working).

Appearance

On the subject of appearance, a word of advice from Janis Penn about how to dress your child for this initial meeting with the agent, 'Don't dress them up for a party, or for a job interview. Don't dress your child with ribbons and fussy clothes. Don't truss them up! And babies mustn't wear headbands. Have them looking comfortable and feeling comfortable. They've got to be natural looking and *clean.*'

N.B. Personal hygiene can be an embarrassing and difficult area for anyone to discuss. Obviously it's difficult if you've been travelling across town with a baby to ensure that its nappy is clean when you arrive. Everyone will be understanding about that. Agencies and everyone else involved in working with babies know to provide a space to allow parents to change or freshen up the child. But basic cleanliness is a must. You could be working in hot, close conditions in studios and if there is a problem with body odour, then everyone will be conscious of it. It is the sort of issue that – no matter how talented the child – will ensure that they never get asked back. 'Personal hygiene is very important,' says Janis

Penn. 'The cutest little toddler came in once for an interview but she was filthy and so were her clothes. That sort of thing is very tricky for us to handle. It's very important to be clean.'

Your child doesn't have to wear the latest fashions, and if you are living within a limited budget, you won't be expected to go out and buy brand new clothes for your child, but it's vital that you always present them at interviews and castings, clean and fresh.

Choose clothes that reflect your child's character, the sort of clothes they are happiest in. Simple clothes are fine. If your child is coming from school and wearing school uniform that is perfectly acceptable. Remember that most acting and modelling jobs for children are looking for 'the child next door'. There is no need and very little point in dressing your child up in anything fancy or unusual. It will not make your child stand out and will only attract the wrong sort of attention.

Janis Penn advises, 'Young lads shouldn't wear suits. A terrific boy aged 13, came to see us last year ... casual, trendy. He went off to get his folio done himself and when we got his photographs, he was wearing a suit. He didn't get a job all year. We put different photographs up on the Internet without the suit and we were able to show clients that he was a fun youngster and suddenly he started to get work. When people come with their children, we tell them how they should prepare them. Casual, comfortable, clean, and youthful – that's the best advice we can give.'

In short, both you and your child want to appear as natural and unaffected as possible.

A special warning

Don't put make-up on young girls. Agents and other professionals in the business want to see your child at their most natural. Anyone looking for a six year-old, wants to see a six year-old. People who want a ten year-old for a job, want to see a ten year-old. Nobody wants to see a child with make-up on. 'And don't dress them as teenagers if they're only six years old!' says Janis Penn.

Rachel York, a former child model, now working in a child model agency, says, 'It isn't like the beauty pageants in America, where you're dressed up and made up and you have to behave and stand a certain way. For this business, they want kids. They don't want mini adults. They *do* want kids.'

Janis Penn says, 'We've had 14 and 15 year-old girls turn up with full make-up when they come in for the interview. We're pretty strict with the mums. We'll say, "You can go into the loo and take all the make-up off. So we can take photographs of a 14 year-old". Often they get pretty shirty with us. But if people want a 19 year-old, there are plenty of real 19 year-old models out there. They don't want a 14 year-old made up to look older. One child's mother grumbled quite a lot about it, but we went ahead without the make-up and the girl has worked all year long. This year that particular mother has brought her other two children in to join the agency.'

Attitude

After the way your child looks, what counts is how they behave when they make their entrance. Be careful about telling your child to be 'on their best behaviour' as this may make them feel inhibited and make them withdrawn. An agent wants to be able to see your child's natural personality as this is what advertisers and photographers will be hoping to capture.

Try to keep your child relaxed and happy. Janis Penn says, 'That first impression is quite important. You know from that first impression – as soon as they walk through the door – whether or not they've got what it takes.'

But don't despair if your child is having an off day or is a little overwhelmed by their first trip to an office for an interview. Janis Penn admits, 'Sometimes, one can slip by, so we know we've got to keep our eyes and ears open to be on the look-out for everything. Sometimes children are a bit inhibited in front of their parents and they won't talk. In that situation, I might say to the mum, "Why don't you go and freshen up after your journey?" Then I'll take the opportunity to have a chat to the little one. If that works, I'll explain privately to the mum later, "When you go in to a casting, stay well out of the way, don't even be within eyeshot."'

Photographer Daniel Pangbourne is familiar with this situation, 'A lot of children work a lot better when their parents aren't there, or when they can't see that they're there. Then they're not playing for their parents, and often they're a lot more confident when their parents aren't watching them. It's funny, parents drop their kids off at school and don't worry about them, but sometimes in the studio they want to start mollycoddling them and if the kids can see that, it inhibits them.'

It isn't just your child's potential which is being measured at an interview. If you're bringing your child along to an agency, be prepared, *you* are going to be scrutinised as much as the child. Agents are looking for a level-headed, practical parent, who can convince them that they will take the work seriously. You will also have to convince them that you are trustworthy. Agents depend on the parent to get the child to a casting or a job. They can't afford to take risks. Janis Penn explains, 'We speak to the parents for about half an hour because they're the ones that will be doing all the hard work. We interview the parents because it's their role that's really important. An ideal parent is one who is obliging, who doesn't get too flustered. They've got to keep a level head. They've got to keep their child's feet on the ground. They've got to try not to spoil them.'

Most professionals say that the first thing that puts them off a child is a star-struck or pushy parent. Janis Penn agrees, 'If a parent is pushing a child into it for their own reasons and the child doesn't really want to do it, then the child just isn't a suitable candidate. We always ask the children, "Whose idea was it to come along today – was it mummy's idea – or was it yours?" Sometimes they'll say, "Mummy wanted to do it." And you know to look very carefully into that. Sometimes you'll have 10 or 11 year-olds who make it very obvious that they are not interested. Sometimes the children are just painfully, painfully shy and you can see it upsets them. Shy children, or simply Not Interested, you really can't do anything about – it's just in the nature of the children.'

If the agent begins to talk directly to the child, it's important that parents sit back and let the child answer for themselves. Janis Penn warns, 'Parents *must* keep out of the interview when we're chatting to their children. They mustn't answer. They have to try to keep quiet and let the young ones do the talking. That can be a common problem. I've lost count of the number of times I've had to say, "No, I'm talking to Johnny, let *him* tell me how he got on at school today!" We have to hold the parents back. Often we take the children into a separate room. We all teach our children that they mustn't go off with strangers, but in this situation, we say to the mother, "You sit there for a moment", and we say to the child, "Just come through here with me." And we wait to see if they will come with us. If they *will* do it, then that's it, they've passed that test.'

But not all agents will take the time to coax an unwilling child. Even Janis Penn admits that the ones who make the best impression are the ones who are keen from the start. She says, 'You're looking for a child that walks in the door and makes eye contact immediately. The ones who look as if they're just about to jump on you, they're so keen!'

How do you tell if an agency is a good one?

Not all agencies are above-board and reputable. It's difficult to tell much from an entry in The Yellow Pages, or on a website: but if they have a prominent presence on both then it is a good start. It means that they will be found easily by companies who are looking to employ child models or actors. Here are some simple checks you can make yourself.

Word of mouth

There is nothing better than personal experience. If you know any other mothers whose children are models, then their recommendation of an agency will be something you can trust. Alternatively, phone around big companies who use child models, such as catalogues or magazines and ask them which agencies they use. At least that way, you can be sure that an agency is in the habit of getting children work.

Trust your own first impressions

When you are invited for an interview at an agency, you will be able to check its premises, and establish that they are in business. First of all, when you telephone the agency, does the person who answers the phone say the name of their company? If not, you should be on your guard. Is your interview going to be held at the address which appears in the Yellow

Pages? Again, if not, you should look in to the agency further. It may be that your interview is being held at other premises for a good reason, but there are common scams involving fake agents, so you must be on your guard.

Ask Questions
It's important that you use the interview situation to ask questions about the running of the business.

The questions to ask an agency
Ask how long they have been in business
A well-established agency which has been around for a long time will have had time to build up a good reputation and connections. On the other hand, while there might be a risk involved with a new, young company, there may be advantages to being taken on by an agency which is hungry for work. The choice is yours. A lot will depend on the impression they make on you.

Ask about their expertise
Find out who they have worked with and what sort of contacts they have among casting directors for photographic work, or for film and television. Take a note of the names of their contacts and if you have serious doubts about the agency, you can check with these other professionals.

Ask what types of jobs they generally find for children
Refer back to the list of modelling and acting jobs available for children in Chapter One and go through it with the agent. Ask if they are known for specialising in certain types of children or certain areas of work. Ask which types of work they mainly deal with (i.e. do they get primarily photographic work for fashion catalogues or magazines, or do they get TV commercials, or television and film drama?). Make sure that the agency is equipped to give you the right representation for your needs. If your child particularly wants to act, but the agency deals mainly in photographic work, then you may want to talk to another agent.

Ask how much competition there is for your child

Find out how many children are in the same category as your child in terms of age and appearance. If the agency has a lot of children of the same look, the chances are reduced of your child getting a lot of work. Most good agencies will try to avoid this, and go for the biggest variety of children possible, as Janis Penn explains, 'We don't want to overload the book with any one age group or type or colouring. We have got to give ourselves a good cross section and choice. For example, for each age group we've got girls, boys, dark hair, blond hair, red hair, Asian, Oriental, mixed race, West Indian, blue eyes, brown eyes, very pretty, very "character", and everything in between! You have to have more than one of each, because you have to be able to give a client the choice. The more choice we have, the more our clients are likely to come back to us, because they know we're able to find what they're looking for. Sometimes parents might think we take on certain types of children because there's a big demand for them – but you never know what someone is going to want. You take on as many different types of children as you can so that there's a good variety to choose from – it's the same as a shop. This is a shop window, for everything from babies up to young-looking 21, 22 year-olds.'

Ask which casting directors or production companies the agency is used to working with

Take a note of their names, and don't be afraid to call them up and ask their opinion of the agency. Find out if the agency has a good reputation within the profession.

Ask what the staff-to-model ratio is

In other words, ask how many children they have on their books and how many staff they have. An office manned by just two people will not be able to handle much work – that's all right if they are concentrating on just a few clients, but it's not okay if they have a couple of thousand clients to try to look after.

Ask to see a portfolio of the agency's work

Tell them you'd like to see what sort of jobs the agency has done in the past. All agencies will be able to produce evidence of the work their models have been involved in. This allows you to see what kind of jobs they've done and the calibre of the clients.

Ask to see their model book

Examine the quality of the book. A high-quality, well-produced book is important. It reflects the standing of the agency within the industry. Flick through it and see if you recognise any faces. Ask the agent to point out some of their more well-known clients.

Ask how many copies of the model book are sent out to professionals in the business

Good distribution is important. The more books which are out there on the desks of casting directors, production companies, magazines and photographers, the more work will come the agency's way.

Ask what methods, other than the model book, they will use to promote your child

They might have a strong Internet presence for example. More and more professionals booking children are communicating via the Internet. If the agency uses a website for promotion, try and get access to a computer to check out their presence on the web.

Ask what costs will be involved

Find out how much it is likely to cost you for photographs and representation, and how much commission the agency will charge. They will normally take a percentage of your earnings, which can be anywhere between 10 and 30 percent.

Finally, if you don't feel comfortable with the agent or the agency, don't sign up

It's important to get on well and feel at ease with an agent. Your relationship with an agent is one that will be based on mutual trust.

Ways of going it alone without an agent
Drama classes or youth theatre groups
Many highly successful performers have never had any formal training, but others got their first breaks through performing in youth theatre. Whether you are going to be represented by an agent, or thinking of going it alone, considering taking classes for singing, dancing or acting might be of benefit to any child who wants a career on the stage. As well as 'learning their craft', they will get the opportunity to mix with other children who share their interests and dreams. The schools will often have performances of shows which give youngsters the experience of being on stage and the chance to show their talents off. Youth theatres and well-respected private dance or drama teachers are often approached by companies holding auditions or looking for leads or extras who require specific talents (i.e. dancers or singers).

Stage schools
This more formal approach involves taking a child out of the normal school system and sending them to a stage school where, in addition to 'normal' school classes, they will get an education which leans heavily towards the performing arts. But they are not suitable for everyone. Hazel Bell considered taking Aidan out of ordinary school and putting him into a stage school, but decided against it in the end. 'Very expensive,' she says, 'and adds tremendously to travel problems. We were very unimpressed by the one we visited.'

Open auditions
Very occasionally, a highly publicised open audition will be announced in trade papers like *The Stage* or in the general press. It might be for a part in a boy band, or a girl band; for a part in a stage musical, like *Annie*; or for a major role in a big budget movie. Normally this is a publicity stunt for the producers, as it guarantees media coverage showing the queues of thousands of hopefuls winding their way through the streets outside

the audition venue. If the opportunity comes up, and the part is tailor-made for your child, then it is just possible that they will be the 'one in a million' (or at least one in several thousand) who wins the part and launches a successful career as a result. Think of it as being very similar to playing the lottery: not to be relied upon to earn a living, but someone has to win, and it could be your child. Bags of patience, a picnic hamper and a camping stool for waiting in very long queues are essential.

Talent contests
These can be a useful method for getting exposure. It's possible – depending on the location of the contest – that talent scouts or managers are present. There will generally be prizes involved, which are worth winning.

Venues can range from fully-equipped theatres with live accompaniment, to small bars and clubs with an audience which is not necessarily attentive and is more concerned about getting their next drink from the bar. There will usually be a series of heats, followed by a final, and at the very least this will provide a young performer with the valuable experience of performing in front of a live audience.

CHAPTER THREE CHECKLIST

Ten tips for attending an interview with an agent
1. One or both parents can attend, but don't take more than one child, unless the agent is considering them.
2. Don't dress the child up as if for a party or for a job interview.
3. Children should look and feel comfortable, dressed casually.
4. Children must be clean.
5. Children should not wear make-up.
6. Young girls should not be dressed up as teenagers – they should look and dress for their correct age.
7. Keep the child relaxed and happy.

Remember parents will be scrutinised too ...
8. Parents must be level-headed, practical and trustworthy.
9. Parents must not be star-struck or pushy.
10. Parents should sit back and let their child be themselves and never butt-in or answer for the child.

Ten questions to ask an agent
1. How long have they been in business?
2. What types of jobs do they generally find for children?
3. How much competition is there for your child?
4. Which casting directors or production companies is the agency used to working with?
5. What is the staff to model ratio?
6. Can you see a portfolio of the agency's work?
7. Can you look at their model book?
8. How many copies of the model book are sent out to professionals in the business?
9. What methods, other than the model book, will they use to promote your child?
10. What costs will be involved?

If you don't feel comfortable with the agent or the agency, don't sign up.

CHAPTER FOUR
There is a Sucker Born Every Minute
How to spot the people who would take advantage of you

Scams

The child modelling and acting business attracts many unscrupulous individuals who see the opportunity to profit from vulnerable parents and children. Anyone can advertise in a newspaper or set up a website claiming to be an agent and offering to find work for models and actors.

The stronger your own ambition, or your child's ambition, the more at risk you will be of falling for an apparent offer to help you to get started. There is nothing more certain than the fact that greed makes people easy prey for confidence tricksters who come with promises of easy money.

General rules

■ Keep a level head and don't let ambition or promises of a fortune to be earned run away with your common sense

■ Never hand over money to anyone without making certain what you will be getting for it

■ Never sign anything without taking the time to check everything very carefully (use a lawyer in the case of contracts with recording companies or managers)

The warning signals – when to be on guard
Agencies who charge higher than average fees for interviews

Check with several agents and see what the 'going rate' is for an assessment. Be very wary of agents who charge very high fees for a simple interview. Be sure to ask the agency what the fee is for. Never pay any sort of fee to an agency with questionable credentials. Refer to the section *How do you tell if an agency is a good one?* and *The questions to ask an agency* (Chapter Three), to check them.

Note: Most agencies will say that because of the huge number of applications they receive, charging a fee protects them from time-wasters and establishes whether or not a parent is serious as well as covering administrative costs. It is not unusual for people in business – from plumbers to lawyers and accountants – to ask clients to pay for their time and expertise. A fee may cover an agent's time for assessing your child and giving you their professional advice. The fee may also include extras, such as photographs. If the agency is otherwise reputable, you will have to judge for yourself whether you feel the fee is worth paying. Some agencies make a point of advertising that they charge no fee for interviews, but they then may go on to trap you into an expensive and unnecessary photographic commitment.

Agencies who insist that you use an expensive photographer

Beware of agencies who insist that you use their own 'approved' photographer. This is another method used by unscrupulous individuals to make money out of parents. Parents agree to it and then discover that the photographer charges very high fees. Children grow and change so often that an elaborate and expensive session with a photographer to produce a folio for a child is completely unnecessary. Above all, remember that with the use of the Internet and model book, no child nowadays requires a large number of costly, glossy photographs, so never hand over money for a large stock of photographs which may never be used. The practice of sending individual photographs out to clients to promote the models on their books is being replaced by the much more effective model book, backed up by Internet promotion, where an image of a child, held in the computer, can be e-mailed to a client in seconds.

You should also never be forced into going with one photographer without a choice. Ask the agency to specify the type of photographs they require, then do some research. Phone and ask other photographers what they would charge to produce the same quality and style of work. Then check for yourself the quality of the photographs they produce, and the price, before committing yourself to anything.

Note: If you want your child to get work, their face must be seen. This means that you *will* have to provide photographs for the agents. Agencies will demand a high standard of photographs and may have a 'house style' for their model book. They will want to guarantee that they present a high-quality, professional image of the company to producers, casting directors and advertisers. However, if an agency recommends a photographer, the price should be competitive and should cost no more than any other professional photographer for the same quality of work. In fact, there is an argument to be made that it should cost less, as the agency should be in a strong position to negotiate a reduction for putting so much business the photographer's way.

Agencies who ask for a fee to represent you

You should never pay a fee simply to have your child represented by an agent or to be 'taken on their books'. Never hand over money without being absolutely sure what it is for. Remember that agents will take a percentage of your child's earnings, and that should be how they make their money.

Note: A controversial area is the model book. There may be a charge to appear in this, but bear in mind that it remains in circulation all year. In the long run, this is much less costly than providing photographs for every potential job, and ensures that your child is seen by many more people in the business. It's important that you weigh up the costs yourself on this matter. A place in the model book may be cheaper in the long run than having to provide several hundred high quality photographs.

Offers of 'training courses'

Be suspicious of agents who suggest or insist that you take a modelling or acting course, especially if it is run by the agency itself. Check the credentials of the person leading the course and make certain that this is not simply a money-making scam which will do your child little or no good.

Note: Attending drama groups or acting courses run by reputable drama teachers or theatre professionals can be beneficial to your child.

Internet scams

Be suspicious of agencies which exist solely on the Internet. Check to make sure that there is a listing showing their office premises and telephone number – if possible, visit their premises and see for yourself that they are a working agency.

Some Internet companies offer to put your child's photograph up on their website for a fee. They make unrealistic claims about the sort of work that will come your way if you do this. There is much more to running a child or adult agency than simply putting photographs in the public domain. Genuine child agencies are personally involved with industry professionals on a day-to-day basis and perform a variety of services (see *All about how an agency works* in Chapter Five).

Note: No reputable agency would take your child on without meeting them. If you send photographs of your child to a company and they offer to take your child on without a face-to-face meeting, do not hand over any money to them, the chances are that they are not a bona fide agency.

Some of these companies do not even claim to be agents or to run agencies. They are quite open about the fact that they are just giving your child a presence on the Internet and they make claims about how much work your child could find as a result. While it is true that many established agencies are using the Internet to promote their models, and an increasing number of casting directors and producers are using the Internet to view pictures of models and actors: it is highly unlikely that anyone would book models or actors through anything but an established agency.

Never hand over money simply to see your child's photograph appear on the Internet. If that is all you want, it can cost practically nothing to set up your own family website with some Internet Service Providers.

Also be careful about 'e-books' offered on the Internet, claiming to be packed full of information. An e-book is an electronically reproduced 'book' which is sold as a file which you download to your computer. Until you download the book you have no idea what size it is, or what sort of information it actually contains. Many are nothing more than pamphlets and can be much more expensive than a traditional book.

Approaches by strangers

If you are approached in a public place by someone claiming to be a talent scout, a photographer, or an agent, be on your guard. A reputable agent will not normally be wandering the streets approaching strangers and suggesting that their children could be models. Anything is possible, and there are stories claiming that this actually has happened, but be very wary if it happens to you. Never arrange to take your child for a photographic session with a stranger. If it seems like a genuine offer, take the time to check to see if the photographer is in the Yellow Pages, and never arrange to meet anyone 'away from the office'.

If your child is performing live somewhere and, after their performance, you are approached and offered a contract with a manager or a recording company – don't sign immediately, even though it's tempting. Check the company out – find out who else they represent. Find out if they are reputable. Always get a lawyer to check contracts.

Advertisements in newspapers

As mentioned earlier, anyone can advertise in a newspaper or set up a website. If you see an advertisement inviting applications from talented youngsters and are tempted, check out the credentials of the advertiser.

If the advertiser claims to be an agent, the chances are strong that this is an outright scam. Agents are inundated with enquiries every week. A well-established agency would never have to advertise. There is a possibility that a brand new agency might advertise in order to build up their book of models quickly, but you have to ask yourself if you would want to be represented by an agent who hadn't yet built up their contacts or reputation within the business. It could take them several years to get properly off the ground, by which time, your own child model or actor will have grown up and missed their opportunity.

If the advertiser is a major television or film company and they are auditioning for a show that you have heard of, then you can be reasonably secure that it is a genuine casting opportunity (as well as being a public relations and promotional exercise for the production). But if you have never heard of them, then do some research before committing yourself and your child. Find out if the company actually exists, and what their previous credits are.

Any young person looking for a career in the music world might see advertisements for auditions for a new 'boy band' or 'girl band'. It might be difficult to find out if it is a reputable or experienced management behind the organisation, but try to find out as much as you can. Make enquiries about the set-up.

Note: Never send in money for an audition or for information about how to apply for an audition. Also beware of premium rate telephone numbers (see details later in this section). The thousands of hopefuls who are desperate for their chance of fame and fortune can provide a quick and easy means of earning cash for someone running a scam.

Competitions for beautiful babies, or 'new faces'
Competitions offering prizes in cash or modelling opportunities can appear in newspapers or on the Internet. Some are simply money-making scams. They charge a large entry fee and it doesn't take much to calculate that if they get hundreds of entries from hopeful parents, then even after deducting the 'Prize Money', the organisers can walk away with a hefty sum. If you regard the entry fee as a lottery ticket and are happy to pay it for the chance to win the prize, then perhaps it's a risk you are willing to take. But bear in mind that it won't advance your child's modelling career, and there is no guarantee that the prize money ever finds its way into the hands of the individuals.

Note: Some famous brands or products *do* hold widely publicised competitions to find a new face to represent their company. You know that you can trust the competition if it is being organised by a company you have heard of. You should never have to pay money to enter such a competition.

Modelling road shows
Another scam which you may find either advertised in your local newspaper or on posters, is a notice proclaiming that a 'Modelling road show' is coming to your local area. It may claim to be searching for

talented youngsters for modelling and TV advertising opportunities. You will be invited to go to a venue such as a local hotel, and along with hundreds of other hopefuls you will listen to a long preamble about the sorts of money which could be earned by the lucky children who succeed. You will be offered assessments, workshops, or advice on the business of modelling. Naturally, for all of these services, they will charge a hefty fee. But they will provide little concrete help to get modelling or acting jobs.

Introductions agencies

Similar to the road show, are agencies who advertise and travel around offering a service of 'introductions' to modelling and acting agencies. For a fee, they will take photographs of your child and claim that they will present the photographs to various agents. Some may even 'guarantee' to place your child with an agent. They can charge large sums of money for a few photographs, then there is no guarantee that they send them anywhere. Janis Penn of Scallywags says, 'I've had phone calls from parents asking if I've received photographs of their children from agencies like this, and of course, I haven't. Then they tell me how much they've paid – shocking amounts, sometimes – I tell these parents what we tell anyone who enquires – send in a couple of snapshots with your details. All people have to do is call up any agency and ask how to apply – they don't need to pay anyone to be introduced!'

Premium rate telephone numbers

Never answer adverts which use premium rate telephone numbers (that is, numbers starting with 090). Never get involved with an agency which expects their clients to call them on a premium rate telephone number. You can be kept hanging on the line, and suddenly find that the telephone call alone has cost you £20.

Organisations who publish warnings about scams

Perhaps the cleverest scam of all is perpetrated by organisations which claim to be offering advice about scams and acting to protect models from abuse. You will find information on the Internet and in newspapers offering genuine warnings about the money-making techniques which fraudsters employ.

Some may be genuine, but be very wary when the warnings and advice are then followed up with a recommendation of an agency which you can safely use and trust together with information for potential models and actors on how to apply. Look into these agencies very carefully.

Some are simply photographers looking for business by charging you for photographic sessions and portfolios. Others are new agencies, with no track record of getting work for models or actors. Well established, experienced agencies, never need to invite applications. Every new company has to start somewhere, but your child's modelling career is a very short one, therefore you must be careful about committing yourself to a company which is just establishing itself and learning the ropes. Find out about their contacts and their client list. New companies could take many children on to their books without any genuine chance of finding work for them. Also be clear about what 'up front' charges there will be (e.g. photography) before you sign up.

CHAPTER FOUR CHECKLIST

Three basic rules for avoiding scams

1. Keep a level head and don't let ambition, or promises of a fortune to be earned, run away with your common sense.
2. Never hand over money to anyone without making certain what you will be getting for it.
3. Never sign anything without taking the time to check everything very carefully (use a lawyer in the case of contracts with recording companies or managers).

The warning signals for scams – when to be on guard

- Agencies who charge higher than average fees for interviews
- Agencies who insist that you only use an expensive photographer of their choosing
- Agencies who ask for a fee to represent you
- Offers of 'training courses'
- Internet agencies
- Approaches by strangers
- Advertisements in newspapers
- Competitions for beautiful babies, or 'new faces'
- Modelling road shows
- Introduction agencies
- Premium rate telephone numbers
- Organisations who publish warnings about scams

CHAPTER FIVE
Someone to Watch Over Me
Getting an agent

What happens next?

After you have been to an interview with an agent – assuming that you asked questions about the agency when you were there, and that you satisfied yourself that they are above board and reliable – you will be anxiously awaiting their decision. You will already have decided that if they agree to take you, then you will be delighted to be represented by them. The whole family will be speculating about the possibilities: imagining the jobs that might launch your son or daughter into the limelight, wondering how much money they will earn, thinking of ways to spend it.

If the agency turns you down ...

Prepare yourself for the possibility that the agent contacts you and says that they won't be taking you on. The most common reason for a refusal is that your child lacked self-confidence. Shyness might be something that they get over with time, or with experience. It may be that they need a little bit more experience of meeting and talking to new people, or you may simply have to wait until they are a bit older.

The next most common problem is with the parent. A parent who is too anxious for their child to work would put an agent off. As mentioned in earlier chapters, it is important that you don't appear to be 'star-struck', or pushy, or to have an unrealistic or over-glamorous image of the world of modelling.

The first thing to do is to try to look objectively back at the interview. Think about the impressions you might have given the agent. Look at ways which you might improve or give a better impression, next time around. After all, having been through one interview, both you and your child are now more experienced – you should be able to build on that.

Even if you're sure that the above reasons don't apply to you and that you can't improve next time around, you mustn't be too disappointed or disheartened. It is quite possible that you did nothing wrong. It could simply have been that when the agent had time to assess your child, they felt either that they had too many other children similar to yours, or that your child didn't fit with what their agency was best equipped to represent.

According to Janis Penn, agencies can become known for representing certain 'types', 'We have clients who say to us — "I come to you for this particular age group because I know you're really strong on this age group." And sometimes they'll mention that they think we're weaker on another age group or type of kid. We like that sort of feedback. We take on board the comments from the previous year and try to rectify things in each new model book that we do.' Therefore, it may be that your child is just unlucky with one particular agency. Janis Penn says, 'It might be that there's nothing wrong with the child, it's just that they're simply not for us, so parents should try another agency as someone else may be after that particular kind of look.'

Being able to deal with rejection is imperative in this business. If you are going to succeed, you will have to learn to cope with it as early as possible. A refusal from one agent doesn't mean that your chances are over. Simply take from the experience whatever you can, learn from it, and move on to the next agent on the list, or wait until your child is a year older and try that agency again.

If the agency offers to take you on ...

If, on the other hand, you receive the phone call or letter informing you that the agent would like to add your child to their books, your first reaction will be to be thrilled at the news. This is what you had hoped for. You have already invested time and money and you are keen to see a return for it. You will want to proceed and get everything underway as quickly as possible.

Now is the time to stop and do some very serious thinking.

Try to resist the temptation to rush into anything. It's important that you understand exactly what you should expect from an agent and what they expect from you. A good agent will sit with you and explain the business and their terms and conditions before asking you to sign anything. Bear in mind that there will be a lot of information to take in at one sitting and you may find everything a bit confusing and overwhelming, especially in the flush of excitement that accompanies being one step closer to your, and your child's, dream.

That is why the right time to do your research is well in advance. Get to know the facts now. It will put you at a distinct advantage if you have a grounding in the business before you go in to sign the contract. This will enable you to ask for details or clarification of any points.

The contract or letter of agreement
Most big agencies will ask you to sign an agreement. Entering into this agreement, if you decide to sign up with the agent, will mean taking a very important step. They will probably insist on 'exclusivity' meaning that you will give them – to the exclusion of all others – the sole right to represent your child. Check it over very carefully. If there is anything you don't understand, don't be afraid to ask the agent to explain it to you.

Don't feel under pressure to sign without reading and fully understanding everything. If you want time to think it over, then say so and take the agreement home with you to examine at your leisure. No reputable agency will force you to sign on the spot.

If it is a verbal agreement that you are offered, ask the agency to put their terms and conditions on paper, in the form of a letter for you, so that you have something for reference. If this is not possible, then you should take a note of the terms and conditions of their fees and commission and ask them how much notice you have to give if you decide to leave; then write a letter to them confirming the terms as you understand them, and send it to them – keeping a copy for yourself.

How an agency works
At its most simple level, an agent uses their connections to find work for your child and in return, takes a percentage of your child's earnings.

An agent provides the liaison between you and the company employing your child as an actor or model. They will negotiate terms and contracts for you and invoice for payment. They are then responsible for paying your child for their modelling or acting work. They will send a cheque to your child, or pay the money direct into your child's bank account after deducting a percentage as their commission, and they will provide statements of your child's earnings.

An agent will protect you from exploitation and will advise you and provide you with all the information you need to look after your child's rights. In return you and your child will be expected to take your professional responsibilities seriously. Janis Penn, 'We explain to all the parents what the set-up is. What they should expect from us: we find them jobs; we invoice for their payments; we receive their payments and pay direct into the child's account; we try to ensure that the child is safe on jobs. We tell them what hard work it can be for them. For example, they might get notice of a casting arranged between 4 and 6pm. If they have other children, they'll have to arrange for them to be picked up and looked after. It can be a hassle for them. From our point of view, the ideal parent is somebody who is going to be there for us.'

You will expect much of your agent, and in return they will have expectations of you. The relationship between an agent and a child's parents is based on mutual trust and commitment. Janis Penn confirms, 'Parents have got to trust that we're taking their children on because we believe we can get them work: and they've got to trust that we will be doing our best to get them that work. We've got to trust them and be sure that they're going to be professional and do their best for us when required. That's really important. Otherwise it can't work.'

Avoiding unrealistic expectations

The phrase 'feast or famine' is never more appropriate than when applied to the child modelling and acting business. Simon Penn explains, 'New models who come on our books – simply because they're presenting a fresh face – tend to get busy to start with. They might get six calls for castings in the first month. And then we can get complaints from the parents because they're getting called out so often. The child's mother will say, "I just can't do all this. I wasn't expecting it." The other side of the coin is, for example, a baby who joined us and got several jobs, with twice as many castings calls in the first two months, then they had a couple of weeks where nothing was happening and the mother wrote to us to say she was very disappointed because the work had dried up! You have to be realistic. Take the work while you can and recognise that it's not always going to be like that. There are going to be times when there's nothing for you. That's just the nature of the business.'

Photographer Daniel Pangbourne agrees, 'It's amazing how some kids become favourites, without anyone actually knowing how or why. They've just "got the look" of that moment – and they'll get used again and again.'

There are no rules about what type of children will be in demand, or when they will be needed. Offers for jobs can come one after the other in the space of a couple of weeks, or you may have to wait for months, hearing nothing. Everything depends on what companies are advertising; which kind of features magazines are running; what drama is being made for television or film. The only thing that you can be sure of is the fact that nothing in this business is predictable. You have to be prepared to wait for a call – perhaps hearing nothing for weeks on end – then be ready to take your child to an interview or a casting at the drop of a hat.

The things you should expect an agent to do for you
Putting your child forward for work
An agent will put your child forward for all the castings and auditions for which your child is suitable. An enquiry for a child might be as vague as 'four year-old boys' or as specific as 'eight year-old girls, blond hair, blue eyes, must be able to play flute and roller-skate'. That's why all the extra information which you can provide for an agent is essential. The more information they have about your child's abilities, the more chance your child has of finding work.

The impression you and your child make at that first interview will determine the types of jobs they will be put forward for initially, as Janis Penn explains, 'We decide from their interview whether they can go straight into the live action jobs – or whether they're going to start out just on the photographic. They have to have a certain type of personality for live work and that has to come across at the interview stage. They have to show that they're competent, confident, and that they'll get the job done. We're very careful when we interview them, we mark down what we believe they're capable of in the first instance.' Your agent's reputation depends on their ability to fit the children to the specifications demanded by producers, photographers or casting agents. Don't expect to be sent along for every job that an agent gets notification of.

Casting Director, Suzy Korel explains how it's best for everyone if the agent gets it right, 'We look at suggestions from the various agents first, before calling the children in. What annoys me incredibly is when the client has said they don't want any red-heads ... and the agent suggests a red-head, or they suggest a child that's the wrong age group. And the big problems arrive if a child is not available, and the agents substitute. It's essential that they pay attention to the brief and send the right type of child. As far as casting directors are concerned, you've got to have a good relationship with the agencies – you've got to know they're not going to waste your time.'

Managing your child's career

An agent will manage and shape your child's career. You will obviously get the opportunity to talk to your agent about the work which your child wants to do and, more importantly, is capable of doing, but it is best to accept your agent's advice. Your agent has vast experience of the market and its demands, they have also seen a large number of children pass through their books over the years and will be a good judge of a child's potential. Never lose sight of the fact that your agent will have your child's best interests as their priority. They *want* your child to get work. They are in business to get your child as much work as they can. If you let them, a good agent will help to guide your child's career.

Photographer, Daniel Pangbourne explains how this part of an agent's job is vital, 'The vetting of a child by the agent is very important. That's why the child and parent will have a meeting with the agent, and that's why they then have a photo session done for the model book. That photo session for the book is a very good indication in microcosm of how a proper job would be done. So it's good for them to do that and to see how it works, and to see how their child works in a situation with professional photographers and assistants and other people milling around.'

Janis Penn talks about an agent's perspective and how they make judgements based on experience, 'We might think: nice child, pleasant manner, good face, will be directed, but they're not very confident. And so we'll decide: let's start them off on photographic, until they're used to being on a set, with strangers, in front of a camera. The experience of doing that will make them more comfortable and build up their confidence. Often that's what happens. From there on, you keep an eye on them. Some will continue just to do photographic work, some will go on to develop and do work for television.'

Rachel York, who used to be a child model and now works at a child modelling agency says, 'We have a five year-old on our books, and the mother felt that they only wanted to do photographic work. But a part in a BBC drama came up, and we felt he could do it. We persuaded them to go along to that, saying, "Just try it and see how it goes ..." Well, he went along to it, and got it, and he loved doing it. Now he goes to acting school at the weekends, and after school. He just knows *that's* what he wants to do from now on – and that's at age five.'

Providing information

It's up to your agent to get all the information you require about a job and pass it on to you. If there is anything that you need to know, ask them. That is what they are there for. Lesley Simpson, whose daughter Tiffany is a child model says, 'When I started out, the agency was really helpful. I could just phone up and ask who? what? where? when? whatever...! And they would always help.'

■ Who and What

They will tell you about the company doing the job and what sort of job you are going for: photographic, television or film. They will give you as much information as they can about what will be expected of your child.

■ Where and When
They will inform you what dates your child will be required and will give you all the details you need about call times and locations of auditions, castings, wardrobe calls or shoots.

■ Wardrobe requirements
They will tell you what clothes you need to provide or if there are any special accessories which you require.

■ Fees and expenses
They'll tell you what sort of fee you can expect for the job, or what expenses are going to be covered.

■ Laws governing the working conditions of your child
Your agent will be able to tell you what hours your child will be expected to work, and what they are entitled to on the different types of jobs which they might get.

Advising on appropriate photographs
Your agent is the best person to advise you on what sort of photographs you need and will often recommend a photographer to take them. A good agent will save you from going to unnecessary expense – for example, no baby needs a folio of professional photographs, babies are constantly growing and changing. Your agent will explain what you require for sending out to clients, for entry into the model book, or for use on the Internet.

Publishing a model book
Most good agents will produce a model book. This is the catalogue which presents the photographs of all the models in an agency. It should show them off to their best advantage in an impressive and practical form.

Using their list of contacts in the business, an agency will ensure that everyone with whom they do business has a copy of their model book delivered to them. In this way, anyone looking for a child model or actor can browse through the photographs at any time and find the children they'd like to interview. A model book is a more effective way to present photographs than to send out individual photographs for a job.

Janis Penn explains about Scallywags' model book, 'Once a year we bring out a book. It's a very glossy catalogue and costs a lot of money to produce, but our clients expect it. We send out 1500 of them to our clients. The model book sits on their reference shelves and is used by them all year long. They can browse through every child we have. The alternative is that every parent would have to provide us with 1500 glossy pictures to mail out – which wouldn't be nearly as effective. Sometimes we bring out a supplementary book to include clients who have joined part of the way through a year.'

When a child starts to get work, the cost of inclusion in the model book will be covered by the money they are earning each year. But taking the decision to find and commit to the money for that first entry requires careful consideration.

There is advice on the Internet and elsewhere, saying that no-one should have to put out money in advance for child modelling. Much of it is well-meaning, but realistically, if you want to promote your child as an actor or a model, it will entail expenditure initially, certainly for photographs. It is worth noting that on close inspection, some people who give this advice – under the pretext of protecting people from scams – are actually photographers, claiming to act as agents, but with a vested interest in getting you to sign up for a photo session and glossy prints. Janis Penn cautions, 'You can spend £500 to £600 on a folio and it's not what anyone wants. The photographs could be mood shots with dramatic lighting etc. Even if the photographs are the right kind, when you send these pictures out to clients, they will get stuck in a drawer; go missing; get detached from the details about the child, and the agency. At the end of the day, it would cost the parent a lot more money to provide us with those prints than it costs to be included in the book.'

If you ensure that you are dealing with a bona fide agency which has a proven track record of getting its models and actors work, then it is up to you to weigh up the risks and potential benefits of any financial investments you have to make.

Ensuring Internet exposure

A good presence on the Internet is becoming essential. Most people involved in the media are doing business by e-mail and on the web. A website can be accessed by anyone, from anywhere in the world. If someone requires to see a photograph of your child, they can view a copy of it in seconds, whilst sitting at their desk.

A website can also be updated instantly, meaning that current photographs with changes to your child's appearance can be registered straight away. This is not nearly as costly as doing hundreds of new prints of your photographs. And if you join an agency late in the year, your child's picture will be instantly accessible, making them available for work immediately.

Negotiating contracts for you

An agent will negotiate contracts and look after your interests. They will be responsible for getting the best deal and checking that the contractual terms are correct. There are many different types of agreements, for photographic work, television and film work, commercials and drama. The rights are complex but a good agent will ensure that everything is in order and to your child's advantage.

An agent will also be on the look-out if your work is used outside of the agreed contract (e.g. if a television commercial is shown beyond the agreed period of time, or if a drama is repeated) and they will pursue the company for the payment on your behalf.

Collecting fees and paying you

An agent will invoice the company for the fee and ensure that the company pays. This is not as simple a task as it may seem. Janis Penn of Scallywags, says, 'We're chasing accounts all the time to get the money out of them. Some of them can take up to a year to pay.'

Simon Penn explains the chain effect, 'We invoice the production company, the production company has to invoice the advertising agency, the advertising agencies are paid by the client – some big shop or company – and everyone has to wait until that money comes through from the top before they can expect anything. Even when the money does start to come through it can take a while to trickle down to us. On average this whole process can take between two and six months. As soon as we receive the money, we send it out to the children with our next payroll. Some clients are very bad. Some of the biggest companies are the worst, claiming that invoices have got lost. Or that it's in the system and being dealt with. That's when you really need an agent. The agents do all the chasing up for you.'

The agent will then pay the money into your child's account, after deducting their percentage. Most agencies pay cheques out to their models in batches or payrolls to rationalise the administration process.

Your responsibilities
Agency fees, percentages
You will have to pay a percentage of your earnings to your agent. Percentages vary, agents might charge anything from 10 to 30 percent, and on top of that there may be additional costs involved for photographs or entry into the model book. Be sure to ask for rates so that you are clear about what to expect.

Personal outlays and costs
Going to interviews
You will be normally be paid a fee to attend a casting or audition. It may only be enough to cover your expenses. Bear in mind that taking a child out for the day inevitably costs more than the transport involved.

Photographs
For tiny babies you should never go to the expense of commissioning a folio from a professional photographer. The baby is changing its

appearance far too quickly. But you may be required to get some good quality shots for the model book or Internet. If shots were taken at your interview, then they should be sufficient. Be sure and ask your agent what they expect.

High quality photographs will be required for older children. Reputable agencies take great care over the presentation of the children on their books. They may require a certain standard and uniformity of style in their model book. Often they will recommend a photographer to use. If the agency produces a high quality model book, and proves that the book generates a lot of work for its models, then you should take their advice seriously. It is possible that the photographer they recommend will do the work for you a better price, but be aware that this is sometimes a scam used by fraudsters to make money (see *Scams*, Chapter Four). To be on the safe side, it would be simple to do a price comparison by calling another freelance photographer and asking for their rate for the job.

The model book
There may be a charge involved for your place in the model book. When working out the value of it, compare it to the cost and efficacy of ordering a large quantity of photographs to be sent out to casting directors, photographers and production companies. You can also compare it to the cost of appearing in *Spotlight*, the standard reference volumes which present photographs and details of professional actors and actresses which are used by casting directors. *Spotlight* produces a volume for children and young performers and charges for each third of a page.

Wardrobe
Obviously for a clothes catalogue or a television or film drama, wardrobe will be provided, but for many jobs, a child is expected to wear their own clothes. This does not mean that a vast array of choice is required. Janis Penn suggests keeping it simple, 'They're best to have T-shirts or sweat shirts in primary colours, plain without logos. Simple. Casual. Sometimes people are looking for school children, in which case they want white shirt, grey skirts or trousers and school shoes.'

It's important that a child's clothes are not emblazoned with logos. If a company is spending a lot of money to advertise its product – they don't want to give free advertising to another company courtesy of a logo which is being featured prominently on a child's top.

Make-up

In general, nobody will be looking for make-up on a child. If make-up is required for a television drama there will be a professional make-up artist on call. They will take care that the make-up they use will be hypoallergenic and safe for use on children.

The only make-up which it might be worthwhile investing in and keeping handy is a 'cover stick' to cover minor blemishes. The rough and tumble of a child's life means that occasional bruises are inevitable and it can be useful to have something available, if required, to cover them up.

Availability

You will be expected to be available at all times unless you have informed your agent otherwise. Opportunities can come up at any time. You will have to be available to go to castings or jobs. Always be prepared to make arrangements at short notice. Janis Penn explains that parents won't just have to be available and prepared to travel to a casting the next day, but there are other considerations, 'They might have to organise a little bit of wardrobe for the children, too.'

In other words, you must be prepared to sort out clothes and laundry before the interview or job: on top of that, there is the possibility of an early rise to travel to the location. It may be inconvenient, but putting in the effort every time you receive a call will pay off in the long run.

In the performance business, if an actor is out of work, this time is called 'resting'. Janis Penn tells parents, 'You can be resting for a long time. You don't know when we're going to phone you again. So try and take advantage of the times that we do phone you. Just try your hardest to get as many castings as you can under your belt. Because the more often your child is out there, being seen, the more often they'll get picked up by people and get other jobs. Once that starts to happen, they'll get known by the clients and will be asked for time and again.'

It won't just be you who is required at short notice: if you have other children who are not involved in modelling or acting, you will have to arrange for a babysitter to look after them, or for someone to collect them from school. This may mean finding an understanding friend or relative on whom you can call, to help out at the last minute.

Janis Penn says, 'If parents have other children, they might have to organise things for them too. That might mean finding a sitter, or rearranging things they'd planned to do. They might have to drop things sometimes for us.'

A parent who makes that extra effort will be appreciated by the agency. If an agent knows they are reliable and prepared to do whatever it takes to get to an interview or a job, then the agent will call them whenever an opportunity arises. Janis Penn says, 'The parents that will do it, and drop things for us, are worth their weight in gold in this business'.

Photographer Daniel Pangbourne warns parents not to underestimate what is required, 'As a parent you've got to be able to take them to all these castings and these jobs, and be reliable. You have to get yourself there at the drop of a hat. Find the place in the A-Z. Get there on time, and do it. And then you might not get the job. Or if you get it, then you have to be available the next Friday for the shoot. You might have to drop everything to do it. It's a big commitment. It's a massive commitment.'

Learning about the business
It would be helpful for you to learn about the business in order to understand how important the part you play in it, is. In time, you will learn by experience, but for the moment, here is an example of how the casting process works.

The casting process for an advertising campaign
A large manufacturer has a product to promote with a deadline for the launch date. Their first step will be for their marketing department to put the product in the hands of an advertising agency. An accounts executive at the advertising agency will work with a creative team to come up with

a concept for an advertising campaign. In order to convey the concept they might devise a script for a commercial which involves casting a family consisting of mother, father and two children.

Once the concept and the script have been cleared by the manufacturer's marketing department, the advertising agency will appoint a production company to film the commercial. A casting director will be brought on board to find a choice of actors from which to cast the family. They may have adult actors already in mind, and in order to choose the right children, they will turn to an agency's model book.

Janis Penn says, 'As far as a casting director is concerned they will look through the book and then phone us up and say, "We're going in to a meeting and we want to put forward certain faces." They'll then go through the book with us, saying: this one, this one, this one, this one, are they all available on this date? And if we say yes, they then go forward to their meeting.'

This meeting may consist of public relations and marketing people plus perhaps a chief executive from the manufacturer; the accounts executive and key representatives of the advertising agency; the producer and director from the production company who will be making the commercial and the casting director. All of these people will be working on more than one project and will have other responsibilities therefore arranging a suitable time to bring them all together to discuss this casting will have been a major administrative job. The date and time of the meeting has probably been pencilled in, well in advance, as part of a tight schedule leading up to, and ultimately ending in, the launch of the product. At this stage, everyone will be working towards a deadline.

Having drawn together perhaps eight or more of the key people involved in the project, they will begin the process of deciding which children to audition or cast. The whole group will examine the photographs of the children. If they have already decided which actors are to play the parents, then an important part of their task will be to match two children up as potential siblings, then to match them to their 'parents'. This is a crucial meeting as it may be their only opportunity to meet together as a group before the shoot for the commercial. When they reach an agreement and make a decision they will get back to the agent and tell the agent which two children have met the approval of everyone at the meeting.

Janis Penn explains, 'Often they'll be going right to the shoot. If they've seen the children's work, they won't necessarily require an audition. So the next step is that we would phone the children's parents up to tell them they've got a booking. Imagine if we do that and one child is okay, but when we say to the other child's mother, "We've got a job for you on Tuesday." The mother says, "Oh dear, we've got a party that day – we can't manage it." What do we do? We have to go back to the client, and say, "We're really sorry, but one of the children isn't available after all." It isn't just a matter of finding a replacement child – it's matching them up with the other child and the actors playing mum and dad. But more importantly – the casting director will have to try to get all those people together again, who were there for the original meeting. Sometimes that's simply not possible to organise. It causes no end of problems. It can be disastrous. And after we've told them the children were all available – it looks like it's all our fault.'

Arranging another meeting to re-cast the children causes problems for everyone, but worst of all is the lasting damage it can do to reputations and relationships. The manufacturer will lose faith in their advertising agent. The advertising agent will blame the casting director and lose faith in them. The casting director will blame the agent and the end result might be that it loses future work for everyone concerned, all down the line.

When you commit to allowing an agent to represent your child, try to bear in mind that it is a professional commitment that you are making. If your child is not going to be available for work, for whatever reason, then it is imperative that you let your agent know as far in advance as possible. It won't affect your chances of future work. On the other hand, if you don't let your agent know until it is too late, and cause the sort of problem described above, your agent will find it difficult to trust you again.

Providing your agent with information
The most important responsibility of all is to provide your agent with

information. Janis Penn says, 'We do try and impress upon parents how important it is to keep us informed about everything. But to be fair, when a child is first taken on, there is such a lot they need to know, and to take in, that it can be confusing for the parents. But what they must do is remember that we're always here at the end of a phone line.'

First, and most obviously, give your agent every detail about your child.

Your child's vital statistics will probably have been recorded at your interview. Most agents will also ask you to fill out a questionnaire about your child's personal details. Be sure to mention any special talents. If your child can dance, swim, play football, or play a musical instrument, then tell your agent. Your agent will keep a record of this with your child's details. Former child model, David York, now working in an agency, gives this advice, 'Parents should encourage their child to be active in all sorts of different things. If a child has more skills or talents it can be really beneficial. Let's say we get a job for a kid that can roller-skate and your kid can roller-skate ... you're right in there – instantly – with a chance. If they can't roller-skate, you're not even on the list. The more things that you can do to a decent level, the more openings there can be for you.' But David adds this warning, 'Special skills are great – but be honest about them, too! It's embarrassing for you, it's embarrassing for us, and it's embarrassing for a casting director, when they've been promised that a kid can skateboard and the kid turns up for the shoot, and clearly has never been on a skateboard in his entire life! We get the call from the client holding us responsible, and asking us to explain what the kid is doing there when he can't skateboard. So never exaggerate!'

You must tell your agent how to reach you at all times

The agent is working every day on behalf of all the children on their books. Their model book is on the desks of professionals all year. Every day, casting directors, photographers or producers who have parts to fill and jobs for children, are browsing through the model book or checking pictures on agency's websites looking for the right face. As long as your child's picture is in the model book or up on the agency's website, people will assume that they are available and ready for work. When a client calls your agent and asks to see your child, your agent needs to arrange an interview to bring you and the client together. As a result, your agent has to be confident that they can reach you at all times. Always leave a telephone number where you can be reached. You will need an answering machine or service. And you will have to get into the habit of checking it regularly. The best answer of all is to have a mobile telephone, but even this is not without its problems. Janis Penn tells all of the mothers of the children on her books, 'It's great to give us mobile phone numbers ... but keep the mobile switched on! More than once, we've found ourselves in the situation where someone wants to book a child for the next day, but we can't get a hold of the mother. It causes all sorts of problems. We might have wardrobe people, stylists, everyone hanging on. The company might need to go out and buy clothes for the shoot, and we just can't get a hold of the mother because her phone is switched off.'

You must tell your agent if anything affects your availability
Your agent's office is taking phone calls all day long from clients asking about the availability children for parts they are casting. They have to be able to answer immediately. Unless your agent hears to the contrary, they will assume that your child is available for work at all times. Janis Penn explains, 'We can't phone up every mother for every enquiry we receive to check if the date is suitable. So we rely upon the mothers to telephone us and let us know when they're not going to be available. We keep all the information on our computer system, next to their details. It's easy for any one of us in the office to pull it up and examine it. Parents have to let us know when they're *not* available; if we hear nothing from them, we assume they are available.'

That means that you must inform your agent if there is anything which would prevent your child from taking a job:
■ If your child has any **illness** or **diseases** such as measles, mumps etc. Take advice from your doctor and inform your agent about how long it will be before they are clear to become available to work again

■ When you book the **family holiday**, make sure that you pass the dates on to your agent

■ If you receive an **appointment** to go to **hospital** or **dentist**, your agent needs to know

■ If there are any **important school exams** which your child would be unable to miss, or big occasions such as **family weddings** or **celebrations**, give your agent these dates

■ In other words, whenever you mark a commitment to go somewhere on a particular date in your diary, be sure to pass it on to your agent at the same time

**You must tell your agent about anything that affects
your child's appearance.**
You will realise by now, that your child's photograph in the model book or on the website is like an advertisement for your child. It is not only a sign to everyone who sees it that your child is available and willing to work; but it should also present an accurate representation of how your child looks. Children can grow very quickly, so the details for **height, shoe sizes** or **clothes sizes** must always be kept up to date.

It's vital that any change of **hairstyle** is reported straight away. Having made a choice from a photograph, a casting director who is looking for a little girl with long flowing hair for a shampoo commercial will be very disappointed if a child with a short hair cut turns up. You will have to supply new photographs as quickly as possible.

Teeth dropping out is another natural hazard for young children. Some advertisers will specify that children must have a full set of teeth for a smile. Others might ask for teeth to be missing. You should inform your agent immediately of any changes to your child's dental situation.

Still on the subject of dental matters, inform your agent if your child has to have **braces on their teeth** fitted. Alternatively, let your agent know if your child has had braces, but is having them removed.

Accidents can happen to anyone. Your agent may not be your first thought when your child falls and **breaks an arm or leg** but once you are back from the hospital, make sure you ring and let your agent know about your child's limited availability. Remember that less serious outcomes of accidents, such as bruises or stitches also have to be mentioned if they are visible. Janis Penn says, 'Clients are expecting what is in the photograph. Parents must inform us of any changes to their children. That means anything affecting that child. We have to be told. There are often calls for nappy shots with babies, so we have to know about cradle cap, rashes, measles, whatever.'

You must contact your agent if you can't make it to a job

If you accept a job, and something happens which means that you have to cancel, tell your agent without delay. No one will hold it against you if your child suddenly takes ill, or there is some sort of emergency which prevents you from going to the shoot. Inform your agent immediately. You will realise by now how difficult it might be for your agent to find a replacement which will be acceptable to everyone concerned. It may be that your child is the only child which will do – in which case, the entire shoot may have to be cancelled and rescheduled for another date. If this is the case, then it will be obvious that you should not cancel for any trivial reason. To back down from a job requires serious consideration.

Janis Penn impresses upon parents, 'It might be fun for you and your child – but for everyone else involved it's a business. Time is money. There's a lot of organisation involved to set up for a shoot. They've got a studio costing perhaps £1000 a day. They've got a photographer. A stylist. The make-up artist. The baby wrangler if there are little children. Not forgetting their *clients*, who've take time out of their busy schedule to come along to the shoot. This is a very, very serious business.'

A leading London photographer recalls just how serious it can be, 'I was involved in a job and the casting was immensely difficult. The client wanted four kids of different race'. It took many hours of searching and auditions to get the right mix of children: not just each of the individual looks and ethnic backgrounds right, but to look at all of them together and get the right heights and the right overall appearance. Once the children were chosen, all the clothes were to be specially made for them (these are called 'samples' in the industry). The shoot was for a campaign to unveil the company's new lines. On the day of the actual shoot. All the children were all supposed to be together for the big group shots. Everyone was there, all the parents and children ... all except *one*. The photographer recalls, 'We kept thinking, they were sure to arrive any minute ... so we waited'. Eventually after phone calls to the agent, back and forth, they finally found out that the child's mother had brought the child to the casting, but she was working the day of the shoot and she'd left it to the father to take the child, but he wanted nothing to do with it. The photographer tried everything to persuade the father to bring the child along, but to no avail, 'There we are ... left high and dry. I've got the client there. We've done the casting. We've hired this massive location. The clothes have been specially made for that kid. We're talking thousands and thousands of pounds ... and no one could do anything. The whole shoot had just been ruined ... So the client says, "Right – who do I sue ... the photographer? The mother? The model agency?"'

The outcome of that situation – just because one child did not turn up – was that the photographer lost an important client, the PR company, because he had organised the casting and had booked the child; the PR company lost a major client, the clothing manufacturer, because they had booked the photographer; and the clothing manufacturer refused to pay anyone. There were hundreds of thousands of pounds of business lost as a result of the knock-on effect of that father who didn't think it was important enough to travel across London to the shoot. He simply didn't understand. So you can see how important it is to go to a job, and only cancel if you have a very good reason.

Janis Penn draws attention to the financial implications, 'If a child simply doesn't turn for a job, we have had clients say to us, "Well, who's going to pay for all this, then?" Our terms and conditions say that we can't be held responsible for a model's conduct.'

It is important to bear in mind that as a child's parent, you are the one who makes the commitment to bring the child to the appointed place at the correct time. At the end of the day, you are the one who is responsible if you don't turn up. People will always understand if a child takes ill. No one can blame you for that. But if you are going to do this, remember, it is a serious business and a serious responsibility which you will be taking on.

You must contact your agent if you are going to be late for a job
Being late can cause as many problems as not turning up at all; but everyone has found themselves, at one time or another, caught up in a situation which is beyond their control. Travel plans can always go wrong. It is possible to get caught up in an unexpected traffic jam, or for a train to be cancelled without warning. As long as you make every effort to be there, people will understand.

What you must do, if you find that you are running late, is inform your agent as soon as you can. Your agent can then contact the people who are waiting for you and give them as much notice as possible. With some warning, they might be able to reschedule and keep themselves busy doing something else until you arrive. Janis Penn says, 'We cannot impress upon parents enough how important it is. If there's any chance whatsoever that they're going to be late they *must* inform us.'

Writer and television producer, Peter May agrees, 'It could be a £3,000,000 project. Scheduled down to the hour. If a kid doesn't turn up when they're supposed to, there could be something like 50 highly-paid professionals, standing around unable to do a thing. All these people are dependent on that child. With a huge amount of money at stake.'

The work done in a photographer's studio is also tightly scheduled, Daniel Pangbourne explains, 'A child might be scheduled for a slot which has been worked out to the minute, which is why you can't be late. If you're late, then that knocks on to the next person. We've had situations where kids have been late and we've had to send them home because they've missed their slot. It's impossible to hold another twenty kids back just for one.'

If you make a commitment to be at a photo shoot, you must turn up at the correct time. You are being paid as a professional for your time and so your whole approach to the process should be professional, too.

After the job, your agent will expect you to get in touch
Your agent requires information from you. In order to invoice correctly on

your behalf, they require to know how many hours you worked at a job. Janis Penn says, 'Parents *must* tell us how long they worked on a job so that we can invoice correctly. Sometimes they don't and we have to chase them up by telephone, and we can't always reach them. We try to negotiate a two-hour minimum for most jobs. If they don't call us with their job times, then we'll invoice for the two-hour minimum. Then the money comes in to us and we pay them, and they say "But we worked for four and a half hours!" And we have to say, "You never told us." And then there's trouble all round. We have job books, which they're supposed to get signed and send in to us. If they don't do that it's important that they tell us by phone. But if they don't let us know how long they worked, all we can do is invoice the company for the minimum.'

Keep a careful note of your hours and take a note, too, of anything which you were surprised by, or unhappy with, which happens on the shoot. Janis Penn says, 'The parent has to be very communicative with us. They have to tell us exactly what happens when they are at a job. If we get feedback, we can help them. If something goes wrong for example, they need to let us know.' So feedback on jobs should include telling your agent immediately if you have had a problem or disagreement with anyone, or you feel that you have been treated unreasonably on a shoot. Don't stay silent. Your agent can only help if they know that something is wrong. It is best to tell your agent as soon as possible, in fact, call your agent from the shoot if necessary. Your agent is your first line in protection – they will act to sort out problems on your behalf, and may even be able to use the information to protect other models.

If things go wrong between yourself and your agent

If you establish a good relationship, based on trust, with your agent, then you should look forward to many happy profitable years together. However it is possible for any relationship to break down.

As with most relationships, problems can often be traced back to a lack of communication. Misunderstandings between people can arise. For that reason, your first course of action should be to discuss any problems with your agent. Don't let resentment build and simmer away if you feel that things are not as they should be.

Arrange for a convenient time to go in and speak in person to your agent.

And remember ... talking to your agent has two main objectives:
1. To let your agent know that you feel something has gone wrong.
2. To solve the problem and find a way to move forward.

First of all, be sure you are clear about these things in your own mind. Ask yourself the following questions and make a note of the things you want to cover in discussion with your agent:

What is the nature of the problem?

Outline briefly what you are unhappy with and why.
- Do you feel that your agent did something wrong?
- Do you take any responsibility yourself?
- Can you explain why you feel it's important?

What can you and your agent do to rectify the situation?

- If nothing can be done, there is no point in having a discussion
- If you are not clear about what you are hoping to achieve, again there is no point in talking to your agent
- If you feel that you should be compensated for something, be clear about what you feel you deserve so that you can identify precisely to your agent what action you would like them to take (e.g. you may only want an apology and an assurance that the same thing will not happen again)
- Have two options in mind: the best you could hope for, and the minimum which you would be willing to accept.
- Think of a concession, something which you could offer to do or agree to in return.

A successful strategy for handling the meeting

Deal with the first point – the nature of the problem – without getting angry or emotional. Don't dwell on recriminations or apportioning blame. If you can take every opportunity you can to accept some responsibility for part of the problem yourself, it will help to create a constructive atmosphere. Once the problem has been aired, shift the focus quickly on to the more important objective of solving the problem and moving forward. If the discussion keeps returning to the problem, you must do your best to keep coming back to finding the solution. Put your suggestions for solving the problem on the table – if possible offer concessions that you are willing to make. You are more likely to reach an agreement if it seems that both you and the agent must be prepared to take positive action.

Above all, remember that it is not productive simply to complain. Remember your purpose: you are there to get things changed for the better. If a solution cannot be found, then your last resort is to consider leaving the agency. But before you take this drastic step, think seriously about the consequences.

It may not be straightforward to find a new agent. If your child has a proven track record as a model or actor, then it should make it easier to find another agent; but there are no guarantees. However, Simon Penn doesn't feel that changing agents reflects badly on the child or parent, 'We just look at the potential of the child. If a kid is working well for another agency, then they should continue to work well.' Your old agent will still be responsible for fees from jobs which they found for you: that means they must continue to pay you and they are still entitled to their percentage. If you move to a new agent, you will go through a period of time where you have two agents invoicing for your work and representing you, which could cause confusion and problems.

If you decide to part company with your agent
First, check your contract, if you have one, and see how much notice you have to give. Take a note of any special instructions or actions which you have to take to terminate your relationship with the agent.

Next, write a letter giving notice of your decision to terminate your contract. Make sure that you comply with the conditions in your contract. Make sure that you put the correct date on your letter and sign it. Keep a copy of your letter.

Either send the letter Recorded Delivery, or take it in to the office personally. You may not particularly want to go in and face the people in the office but it can be advantageous to hand the letter in personally. You can be sure that the letter has been received. You will be able to collect any material which belongs to you, such as photographs or CV's.

Additional ways to help yourself

You don't have to leave everything up to your agent. You can help yourself by generating publicity whenever possible. Whenever your child's face is seen, it can help you get more jobs.

Self-promotion and marketing

Approach your local newspaper. Many local newspapers are happy to run stories about people who live in the area. If your child lands a big contract for work, or wins a competition, or gets a part in a movie or major television drama, your local newspaper will probably be happy to hear about it. It's a good opportunity for a photograph and story. Simply telephone the newspaper and put the idea to them.

Get a website. If you have a computer and access to the Internet, nothing could be simpler than to get yourself a website. Internet Service Providers normally allow their customers free website space, and many of them offer a basic template for you to fill in. It can be as simple a matter as typing in a few details, and sending them some photographs and before you know it, your website will be on-line. By listing the jobs they have done, and the experience and talents they have, you can use the website to promote your child. If you give clear details of your agent – or provide a link to your agent's website – so that people can get in touch, then it's possible that someone might come across your website and decide that yours is the child they need for that big advertising campaign.

CHAPTER FIVE CHECKLIST

What you should expect an agent to do for you:
- put your child forward for work
- manage and shape your child's career
- give you all the information you need
- advise on appropriate photographs
- negotiate contracts for you
- collect your fees and pay you
- most agents will publish a model book
- many agents will ensure Internet exposure

What you will be expected to do:
- pay agency fees, percentages
- be available
- give your agent every detail about your child and keep them updated about any changes
- tell your agent how to reach you at all times
- tell your agent if anything affects your availability
- learn about the business
- contact your agent if you can't make it to a job
- contact your agent if you are going to be late for a job
- tell them how many hours you worked at a job
- tell them if you have had a problem or disagreement with anyone
- tell them if you feel that you have been treated unreasonably on a shoot

CHAPTER SIX
Oh What a Beautiful Morning
Getting an audition

Finally, the opportunity you've been waiting for, the chance for all the dreams to come true: the call from your agent to say that you have an appointment to go to an audition or casting.

Agent Janis Penn says, 'The first audition can be very daunting. Some children are nervous but for others – it's just their scene – they can't wait to get right in there: happy, comfortable, loving the whole thing.' However your child copes with it, they will cope best if you are well-prepared. Before you do anything else, make sure you have all the information – and before you do that, ensure you have a safe place to keep that information.

Be prepared
First, go out and buy
- a loose-leaf ring binder
- a supply of paper
- a supply of transparent plastic pockets with holes to fit the binder
- a supply of card dividers with holes to fit the binder

This will become your source and record of all information.

Keep notes of auditions, castings and shoots, dates, locations, companies involved, contact names and phone numbers by slipping all the paperwork into the plastic pockets. Use it to store information about your fees and expenses (see Chapter Eight for notes on keeping your accounts). Always take a spare plastic pocket out to auditions or jobs and pop receipts into it as soon as you get them. Use the card dividers to keep information about each job separate and you will be able to go straight to the section on the job you are looking for. If you require to check up on a payment that is due, or to find details of expenses for the inland revenue, you will be able to lay your hands on the information straight away, rather than trying to find all the odd pieces of paper from all over the house. Start out with a system like this and you will reap the benefits in the long run.

Take a note of the following questions. Put this list in a plastic pocket and keep it at the start of your binder. Refer to it to refresh your memory whenever you need it. For each audition, write down the answers to the questions, put them in a plastic pocket for protection, and take them to the audition, remembering to file them in your ring binder when you return!

Questions to ask before you go to an audition

When your agent calls you to tell you that your child is being considered for a job, you may be so carried away that you forget to get all the facts. Your agent should tell you everything you need to know, but keep a checklist on hand to make sure that you know exactly what to expect. You must be well prepared in advance so that nothing takes you by surprise and upsets your chances.

What is the date of the shoot?

Before you find out anything about the audition itself, find out about the shoot dates. Photographer, Daniel Pangbourne explains why this is the most important question of all, 'The first question you should ask, as a parent, when you get a casting, ought to be ... "When is the shoot date?" Because if you can't make the shoot, there's no point in going for the casting. A lot of people come to a casting and we say, "Great – we'd like to book you for next Friday," and they say, "But I'm going on holiday next Friday." They didn't think to tell the agency that it was Auntie Maude's birthday and they were going to Scotland that weekend, so they're not available. People don't realise – it takes *hours* of work and effort to set castings up. It's a waste of everyone's time. So always be aware – check the shoot date.'

What is the date, time and location of the audition?

If you are available for the shoot dates, make sure that you are available, or that you can make yourself available, for the casting. If you have to make special arrangements for you and your child to be free, or special travel plans to ensure that you can arrive on time, ask your agent for time to sort things out, then get back to them as soon as possible to confirm.

What kind of job is it, and what type of child are they looking for?

Find out as much as you can about the type of job it is. Is it for a photographic shoot, or something for film or television? What type of child are they looking for? Although your agent should take care to put you forward for jobs which suit your child, it is best if you double check. Make sure that your child fits the requirements. If the company wants a girl with long hair and you have just had your daughter's hair cut, but have forgotten to tell your agent, it's better for everyone to find out before you waste your time going to the audition.

What will be required of your child?

Find out as much as you can about what your child will be required to do and ensure that your child is capable of doing whatever is required. Former child model, David York advises, 'If you're a parent try to find out as much information about what is being looked for. If they're looking for someone who can play football – find out what tricks they might be looking for.'

Be realistic about your child's talents and abilities. Never put them forward for something if they aren't suitable for it (e.g. if the company requires a child to roller-skate – make sure your child is happy and comfortable with that).

Baby wrangler, Cat Sulley says that the requirements for every job are different so it's important to get as many details as possible, 'We had a job recently where we had to have toddlers on grass having a picnic, so we had to have toddlers who were happy to be on grass, some babies don't like the feel of it on their feet. You might have to think about all sorts of things like, has you baby walked on grass before? What will your baby eat? Will they squash a banana? Are they happy to make a mess?'

If it is a commercial, what is the product being advertised?

It's important to ask about the product in advance as you may not wish to be associated with certain products, or your child may have an allergy to certain products.

The audition, casting, or 'Go-see'

Whatever name it is given, the principle is the same. This is the meeting you will be called to, so that a producer, a casting director, a photographer or any combination of them, can meet your child in person and assess their suitability for the role they will be required to play. The form each interview takes will vary. It will be determined in the first instance by the type of acting or modelling job being cast and, secondly, by the age of the child.

Casting directors

Casting directors will often be hired by film, TV and commercial producers to take charge of the casting process for leading or featured roles. Often extras will be cast simply from the list of specifications given to an agent. For major film and television productions, companies may call upon different types of casting directors. Some specialise in finding the leading (principal or featured role) performers while others specialise in background casting, in other words all the extras required for crowd scenes.

Casting for film or television drama, or commercials

There will normally always be an audition for film and television work. The only time a child might not be seen beforehand is if the producer or director knows the child and is sure about what they can do. But even in this situation, the child will normally be called in so that the other people involved in the casting process can have a look and judge for themselves. Agent, Janis Penn says, 'For the film and TV side, drama and commercials, people tend to ask to see children who have had previous acting or performing experience to consider them for a featured part. On the other hand, for extras — and remember, commercials also have extra work or background work — we're sometimes just asked to send children along who fit the bill. In that situation, we can send along children who haven't done it before – new kids on our books – and it gives them a chance to get a bit of experience alongside kids who know the ropes.'

Casting for photographic shoots
Casting directors will also be hired by advertising agencies to choose children for a photographic shoot, often working together with the photographer in the decision about which children to see at a casting and which ones to use on the eventual shoot.

Photographer Daniel Pangbourne describes the process. 'When a client comes to me they might say that they want dark-haired five year-old boys and blond-haired eight year-old girls. I'll either suggest from the model books ones that I think will be right, or I'll ring the model agencies and get them to e-mail me with details of *every* five year-old boy with dark hair and *every* eight year-old girl with blond hair that they've got. They'll e-mail me all the pictures. I'll put them all together and e-mail them to the client; then they'll pick the ones that they want to come to the casting. So, out of say, 50, we'll pick ten favourites to come to a casting, which we do in the studio. We'll get them to do more or less what they would be doing on the shoot to see if they can do it. Then we'll look at those images at the end of the day and pick our favourites for the actual shoot which might be one day later or one week later or whatever. So it's very much a combined effort between the client and the photographer – deciding who's right for the job, who's got the right look. You can't always tell from the model book. Generally, from a casting point of view, choosing a child is a group decision.'

Financial Reimbursement
There is usually a casting fee for jobs in the advertising field. It may be enough to cover your expenses. However, in television, theatre and film, children are treated like adults. In other words, no fees are paid for attending auditions or castings, but if the child gets the job, then they will be paid Equity rates.

How you and your child should approach the casting or audition

A relaxed, happy, confident child is more likely to do well at an audition. Your approach will influence your child's frame of mind so now is the time to take great care about the attitude you take. Most parents recommend treating the outing as a day out. Casting director, Suzy Korel says, 'It's all down to the attitude of the parent. If they decide it's a fun day out for the child and actually bring in a colouring book to keep the child occupied when they're not required, that's great.'

Mother of two model girls, Donna Hearn says, 'When they were younger we'd go out on a boat after an audition and make a day of it for them, but we don't do that as much now because they're so used to it. They take it in their stride. They know they're going for an audition, or that they're going to do a job. Becky likes to tell everyone, "I'm going to be on the TV!". But Charlie doesn't even bother telling people.'

Lesley Simpson tries to take a light-hearted approach with her daughter, too, 'We have a trip to London. A nice day out. Tiffany goes to an audition. She enjoys it. She comes home and we don't think any more about it. It's like a treat – the whole day out. I just encourage Tiffany to forget about it afterwards.'

What is the procedure at an audition or casting?

The meeting can be anything from a 15 minute chat with you and your child, to a much longer session where the child will be asked to go through some of the motions that will be required from them on the shoot. Photographs will probably be taken, perhaps even a screen test with a recording on video. Young children may be asked to play games to see if they can accept direction. Older children, going for a part in a drama, may be asked to read something from the script.

Casting director, Suzy Korel, explains her procedure with young children, 'I get them all to say their names and to tell me what they like doing, and whether or not they've been on television before. A lot depends on the age group. We usually sing songs or play games. I might get them to tell a joke, tell a secret, or discuss a birthday or a holiday ... pretty standard things that you would expect, to try and get a child to chat.'

Television producer, Peter May, also starts by chatting to the child, 'You can tell a lot from simple conversation. So many kids have nothing to say at all, you have to drag monosyllabic responses out of them. If that's the case, you know you can't use them. I would be looking for a child who listens well and who can engage you with their reply in return. That quality of interacting reflects a child's ability to act. Once we've established that a child can do that, we would call them back for an audition where we would give them a script, and get them to play a scene. That way you can see how they handle someone else's words, and see if they can take direction.'

What will be expected of a child?

Very young children will have little awareness of what exactly is happening. Everything will depend on them having the right temperament at the required moment. But do be aware that suddenly being placed in an alien environment with a lot of strange faces could be a frightening experience. Children of any age could be over-awed by it.

Former child model, Rachel York remembers, 'As a kid you're thrust into an completely unfamiliar place. It can throw you – and scare you. There are loads of other kids you don't know around you, and loads of people bustling about. Suddenly you're called up and told, "Stand up. Stand there. Smile". So you smile. Then they take your polaroid. Then they say "Do this. Do that. Fill in this form. Walk through to that room. Go to that camera. Smile. Say your name. Do this. Do that. Thanks. Bye bye." And by the end of it, you're left thinking ... "What just happened, Mum ... What happened?" For the first few times, most kids are thinking, "Where am I? Who are these people?" It is going to take them a little while to get used to it. But you really do get used to it. After a while, you relax, and think, "Okay, now we're going have our picture taken. Now we're going to do that ... and that ... and that's fine, I know what I'm doing." You start to take it in your stride. Some kids adjust to it straight away. They go along and they get their first job – just like that. But when I talk to the mums, I try to explain to them that it's a completely new situation to their kids and they have to be there to reassure them.'

Most children quickly realise what the auditions are all about, and in no time, will be playing the game like professionals. Rachel's brother, ex child model David York recalls how he got used to the procedure, 'You know that you're going to go in and they'll sit you down, and they'll ask you some questions, or ask you to do a certain thing. And you know they don't want to draw a blank – that you've to keep them happy. So you say to yourself, "Okay, so what do they want me do?" They might say, "Try to look surprised." So you pull the "surprised" face – as if you've just seen Dracula walking down the street. And they might jump back and say, "Whoah – we didn't mean that surprised!" So you give them the "slightly less surprised" face, like, "Oh look there are no unusual bits of anything on my toast at breakfast time ... that's a nice surprise ..." Sometimes you need a little bit of guidance, it's a matter of finding out what they're looking for.'

What is the interviewer looking for?

The most common characteristics which interviewers mention are self-confidence, a happy, outgoing manner and an ability to follow directions. Shy, retiring children or, at the other end of the scale, disruptive, disobedient and difficult to control children will not be suited to this sort of activity.

Casting director, Suzy Korel, says she is looking for several things, 'Confidence. How disruptive they are with other kids. How they interact with other kids at the casting. But all those things are really incorporated with whether or not the child wants to be there.'

Photographer, Daniel Pangbourne, stresses the importance of that, 'A lot of kids simply don't want to do it. Sometimes you realise it's the parents who want the kids to do it, rather than them thinking the kids would be good at it, and want to do it, and would get a lot out of it. That's the big difference. Sometimes you see the parents living their life again through the child.'

A *warning note for parents*

Parents can influence a casting director's decisions about a child. Suzy Korel says that as far as she is concerned, there is nothing worse than a parent trying to force an unwilling child into an audition. 'The ones who insist on their children doing it when their children obviously don't want to do it. The ones who say, "We've come all this way, if you don't do it, you won't get this, or you won't get that." At the end of the day, it is all down to what the parents are like.'

So remember that you will be under scrutiny as much as your child, at an audition. You are there as a chaperone, to look after your child, and represent their interests; but when you do that, you should be supportive and discreet. Professionals working on a shoot will be put off by parents who appear interfering or demanding. Photographer Daniel Pangbourne says, 'There's too much going on to deal with difficult parents on top. There's so much riding on a commercial job. Not just financially, but career-wise and agency-wise, you have a million other things to worry about. So you want to take out all the possibilities of something going wrong. And if you see something in a parent – the possibility of them causing problems or interfering – then it's not even worth entering that into the equation. It's really important to choose the people correctly. On the other hand if the kid is brilliant, you may work out a way around a difficult parent.'

Mother of model Tiffany, Lesley Simpson recognises the danger signs in other parents, 'The parents who become too pushy or too full of their own children – or whose children are too full of themselves – are the ones who won't last. I remember one audition, where a boy came in and looked around the group of parents and kids waiting, then turned to his father and said loudly, "Well, I should get this job easily, shouldn't I?" All of us other parents and children in the room just exchanged looks of disbelief! It was a very poor attitude. A child like that can only have disappointment ahead of him. Parents need to keep their feet on the ground. If parents get too high aspirations, and the kids do, too, then ... well, it might pan out all right for them; but let's be honest, there are an awful lot of kids out there all doing the same thing. A lot of competition. It's more likely to go wrong for them in the end.'

Baby wrangler, Cat Sulley, who works with photographers, has a special warning for mothers of small babies, 'If you're very protective of your child, don't do it! If your child doesn't enjoy doing it, stop doing it! If the baby doesn't want to do it, it's unfair on the whole team that's trying to work with it. It might be very tempting to push if there's a lot of money involved. But it's not worth it.'

What makes a good impression?

Assuming that children fit the physical requirements of a job, energy and enthusiasm will be the first characteristics to catch the attention of interviewers. An engaging personality will come across better if the child makes good eye contact and if older children have the ability to chat easily they will be at an advantage.

Rachel York now working for a model agency says, 'If we've got a brief for a blond-haired, blue-eyed, four year-old, and we send along four blond-haired, blue-eyed, four year-olds, perhaps two of them turn up full of energy, and two go in, timid. I know that the really boisterous kids will have the best chance. Even if they are verging on the annoying! The confident, loud kid will get the job. Because on the day of the shoot, when they need that kid to have the energy – jumping about, really enjoying themselves, looking like they're having fun – then everyone knows that that kid will do it. So, part of what's required is the right look, and part is confidence. It's easier to calm a child down than to gee them up and get the energy out of them. We look for the kids with energy, who'll talk to anyone.'

Casting director, Suzy Korel admits that sometimes a child can be difficult to handle if they have too much energy, but she says, 'When I know that there's a child who's always completely wild, but fantastic, I have to warn the director. Sometimes I have to hold the child by the shoulders, and make him look me in the face to calm him down. But that's all part of the casting director's job.'

Television producer, Peter May, says that when casting a child actor for a part, the first thing he looks for is a bright, confident personality and good eye contact. When he had a major role for a child in the Scottish drama serial, 'Machair', Evelyn Coull made an immediate impact, 'She walked into the room, full of life, with a bright smile and she made good eye contact with all of us, there were three of us, myself and two directors.'

Hebridean Evelyn Coull, now a radio producer, recalls how she came to audition for the role, 'I was around 11 or 12 when "Machair" started filming in my village. It was really exciting to see so many people and vehicles in what was a very remote, lonely village to grow up in. I had never thought about being an actress or wanting to be on television. The week before I read the advertisement in the *Stornoway Gazette* I had just received the award for best actress in school; so I thought, "Go for it!" I had just turned 13 then. My parents were behind me all the way. But on the nights of the auditions, I made my mother go to visit a friend and let me go to the audition on my own. I wanted to do it alone. I think this may have surprised the other doting mothers who were all set on their daughter getting the part! I don't remember being nervous at all, I knew very little about the part I was going for. Maybe I was just that bit too young to really understand what I was undertaking! I just went in there and talked and talked and talked'.

Peter May says, 'Yes, she had no problem talking as I recall! We just made conversation. She talked about a minky whale that had got stranded near to where she lived, and how she had gone down to it every day to see how the progress was going, in the attempts to coax it back out to sea! She spoke intelligently and fluently and in an interactive way. She didn't simply respond to questions, we were able to have a conversation. The next stage from that was to get her to read. We had a short-list of three or four kids who came back on another night. On that occasion we brought along one of the actors from the show, and a scene specially written for the audition: a conversation between the parent and the child. We gave the kids a chance to read it through themselves, before they did the reading with the actor. And at that stage Evelyn was just head and shoulders above the rest. With each of the others, although they had responded quite well in the initial interview, their personalities didn't come across the way Evelyn's did. The personality was the key here for us. There was something in Evelyn's performance, something of herself shining through, and in television that's very important. When she did the reading with the actor she was terrific.'

Former child model, David York, now working in a child modelling agency, shares his secrets of success with children going to castings, 'The client makes the decision, so what you have to do is go in there and make them notice you. Be the best you can be. Be chatty. Be friendly. Look them right in the eye. Shake their hand and tell them, "Hi, my name's Dave!" And be thinking to yourself – I'm really good! And you're going to want me because I'm great!'

What makes a bad impression?
Casting director, Suzy Korel, describes without hesitation, the thing which makes her heart sink at a casting, 'When they bring in their mothers, their fathers, their sisters, their uncles, their aunts, and their friends!'

Remember that you are attending in the professional capacity of chaperone. No one expects, or wants, you to bring along relatives or friends to see how the audition goes. In particular, don't bring along children who are not involved in the audition. Another leading casting director recalls, 'I once had a mother who brought her five year-old twins along with her two year-old who was coming for the casting, and this mother had *no* control over any of them. I had to ring up the agent and say "This family has to come off your books!" You cannot afford to have children like that, who are wild, and a mother who can't deal with them.'

Peter May describes the factors which immediately put him off, 'If you're sitting talking to a kid who a) won't meet your eye, b) has got nothing to say to you and c) can't interact and can only really respond in a very limited way to questions you ask, then there's no sign there of a child who would be capable of play-acting or pretending to react – in other words to act. That's not to say that every kid who can sit and talk to you can act, but a kid who *can't* sit and talk to you will never be able to do it.'

Suzy Korel agrees that a confident, happy child is what she's looking for first and foremost, 'When the child is clinging to the mother and doesn't want to come in, it's no use. The first rule is that the child has to be happy, to think of it as a game.'

Punctuality & etiquette
Arriving on time is not just good manners, it also ensures that you and

your child suffer the minimum of stress. Baby wrangler, Cat Sulley says, 'Be on time. Mum or dad should not be late and rushing around. It's not good for the baby – they pick up on the stress.'

Suzy Korel agrees, and makes the point that being on time, means not being late, and not arriving early, either, 'Sticking to the time-table helps – not thinking, if I turn up half an hour early, I can come in.' She summarises 'My main requirements would be that kids need to turn up on time, with one parent, happy.'

Appearance

You may have been given specific instructions about what clothes are required – if so, you should comply with them. If you haven't been told about clothes, you should ask your agent what sort of look, or image, your child should be putting forward.

David York says, 'If the kid is wearing a suit and tie – that's the image that will stick with the people at the casting. They won't be working at trying to imagine the child in a hooded top with a backward baseball cap. They'll just say "No. That kid's too straightlaced, too conservative."'

If the remit isn't specific, but simply asks for a child of a certain age and sex, then agent Janis Penn advises, 'Remember when you're going to a casting or an audition that you're not going to a party, you're not going to a wedding, you're not going to a job interview. You should just be trying to convey a bit of your child's own personality.'

Suzy Korel says, 'If they're coming straight from school and they're in their school uniform, that's fine. Little girls shouldn't have lipstick or mascara, that just makes them look silly. Kids are kids. Don't try to make little girls look like grown-ups to enhance their attractiveness.'

In the case of modelling or acting jobs for children, remember that ordinary, natural *children* are exactly what people are looking for: and that is what they are expecting to see at a casting. Don't dress your child up as a mini-adult, don't put make-up on your child, and remove any jewellery. Baby wrangler, Cat Sulley confirms this and reminds parents, 'Always take earrings out of young ones' ears before you arrive. We never use jewellery on children.'

Suzy Korel agrees, 'I'm not a great fan of boys with earrings, or other jewellery. Jewellery in general is a no-no. I'm also not a great fan of vast amounts of gel in the hair or bizarre haircuts'.

Cat Sulley makes a special plea to parents of little babies, 'If you have a baby, and they've had a cold, and have snotty noses, try to get that cleaned off before you go in. Wash baby thoroughly before you leave the house. A lot of people have problems with washing faces, or changing nappies – so the more you can do to make their job easier, the better.'

Preparing for an audition or casting

The impression your child makes on entering the room is the one which will have the most lasting effect on an interviewer. Above all, you should encourage your child to be relaxed, smiling and happy.

Janis Penn says 'If you can, go into a place smiling. Many times I've said to mothers, have a little joke up your sleeve. Tell your son or daughter a joke just as you're going in. So that the first thing a client sees is the child animated, laughing.'

David York remembers his modelling days, 'My mum used to tell me, "Now make sure you look them in the eye and be friendly and be nice." I got that sort of advice all the time, but you know, pretty soon, you just start to cotton on to how it all works.'

Children are very eager to please, and it won't be long before your child learns what is expected and what sort of behaviour gets the most favourable reaction. A parent's guidance can help a child to prepare, but only if the parent understands what casting directors and other professionals are looking for. In most situations, they are looking for a child who can be themselves, who can be at ease behaving naturally, and one who is able to portray an average youngster.

Models' mother Donna Hearn says, 'I know of one child and her mother that I've met on a few occasions at auditions. Before they go in, the mother's always making the girl practise her singing. She's got her singing a song, like something out of "Annie", as she goes in. It's just not natural. Most child modelling is about being natural – that's what they're looking for.'

Lesley Simpson, mother of model Tiffany says, 'We've met other mums and kids in our time, and we've seen them at the auditions. The mothers will be fussing, and brushing their child's hair over and over again, and telling them, "Do this – Do that – You mustn't do this – You mustn't do that". But that's not what we're about. I try not to make any fuss at all. We just go straight to the audition, and when I say to Tiffany, "Do your hair," that just means, "Take it out of the ponytail and shake it!"'

David York says, 'Doing drama at school can help. I also did a bit of drama outside of school. But when you're doing commercials, no-one is looking for Shakespeare. It's fairly basic stuff you're called on to do. The sort of stuff you learn from life experience, really. Trouble is, when you're six, you just haven't had that much life experience!'

Encouraging your child to go to drama classes might help to develop their self-confidence, but won't necessarily teach them anything useful in terms of performance. Directors or producers casting parts in theatre, television and film are often looking for children with potential: children who are responsive to direction, rather than children who have had been taught how to deliver speeches by rote or repetition.

Charles Moritz, who wrote and directed for the Manchester Youth Theatre, speaks of the dangers of 'training'. 'It was always sad to see the number of youngsters whose natural presence had been badly compromised by being "schooled" for the stage too young. Whilst a professional training can be of vital importance later on, I think it can lock up rather than liberate talent if taken on too early. On more than one occasion I would see a youngster present him or herself, and when it came time to do their audition piece, they would adopt a stagey pose, and announce the extract in an artificial, modulated sing-song which they would then sustain for the rest of the recitation. I would then try and weigh up whether I thought this was someone it would be possible to coax a true performance from *in spite* of all the work that had been done on them. One of the clinchers for me, however, would be when they came and sat down again for a chat having given their Juliet, Julius Caesar, Lady Macbeth or whatever. We would ask if they had read the play. It was amazing how many times they said they had not. But worse, when pressed if they knew what the story was, it was incredible how often some of these youngsters hadn't got a clue about that either. It simply confirmed for me the fact that they had been put through a process in their tutoring which left them behind in some ways. So, think long and hard about speech and drama exams. Let your child express his or her own enthusiasm for acting and don't impose that on them. Do encourage your child if they have ability and enthusiasm. Youth theatres can be a great training ground. They are, in any case, a very formative experience, and will naturally help young actors decide if they want to go on to use that experience as part of their adult working lives. And finally, if you go for a youth theatre audition (or an audition for theatre, film, or TV) make sure you at least know the story, and preferably have read the script. Those kids who said they hadn't read the play *and* didn't know the story, we would invariably reject.'

Coping with nerves

No matter how excited you are about an audition and the chances it may offer, if a big part or a lucrative contract is the prize, try not to put pressure on your child. Keeping a light-hearted attitude is the best approach. Never make it seem important.

As a mother of a model, Lesley Simpson says, 'In the early days, we would go along to auditions and I would tell her she was just going to see someone, and that she might get her photo taken, and that was it. That was how we approached it. Now, of course, she knows what's going on, but Tiffany is almost blasé about it. She's not nervous at all about auditions. She just says "It's not important whether I get it or not". And that's my attitude, too. She does her best and she enjoys herself. But it's important to me that she mustn't get too stressed about getting a job.'

Keeping a light-hearted attitude

Try to treat the day as a nice day out and don't pin too much on it. With very young children this will be easy. However, as children get older, they will begin to be aware of the difference between an audition and a job. They will soon realise that they are being interviewed and that sometimes they get a job, but at other times, they don't get a job. It will be difficult to prevent them from feeling that they are being rejected. David York recalls his early experiences of rejection, 'Sometimes you would go along to a casting and you think, "I really want to do this job – it looks like so much fun." And you give it everything you've got, and the people at the audition tell you, "Wow – you were great, really great!" So you think you've impressed them, and you're sure you've got the job. But then ... you don't hear anything. So you call up your agent, and you ask if you got it, and they tell you that they're sorry, but no, you didn't get it. You just think, "But what did I do wrong? I thought I did everything right! They thought I was great – they told me so!" It takes a while to sink in, but eventually you start to realise they were just trying to protect you. People don't want to say, "Well actually ... you weren't that great – you weren't right for it." They're just trying to soften the blow, really. So never assume a job is yours. In fact, it helps if you don't get too excited about the possibility of doing a job.'

The key is to take everything one step at a time. If you get an audition, just focus on the audition, and never look any further than that. Agent Janis Penn advises, 'Don't give the child the impression that there's a lot riding on the audition. Don't put pressure on them. You just want them to be relaxed and able to do their best. If it doesn't work, it doesn't work. Next time could be different. Keep them focused on the fact it's fun even to get that far.'

Grabbing opportunities

Work can be very unpredictable. It is impossible to know when opportunities are going to come up. Rachel York speaks about her work in a child modelling agency, 'We have a few really lucky kids. It just so happens that their age group is really busy at the moment. They're always out. They are really busy. Their mums have adjusted their lives to fit all the castings in. But some mums complain, they say, "Well, he's got football on that day, and swimming on that day, we can't fit that one in ..." and we have to explain to them that occasionally he may need to miss a swimming or football session. The mums aren't happy because they've paid for these things. But at the end of the day, it's a question of the parents' priorities. They might decide the football's more important than a casting, especially when a casting's a gamble and there's no guarantee of getting a job. But the kids that are the most successful have the parents that really do get them out there for every available casting. If you're always out – you're going to get *something*. So they have to focus on it – take it seriously – and grab every opportunity that's going.'

Sometimes it's hard for parents and children to keep up the enthusiasm for going along to auditions if they aren't getting jobs. David York says, 'You have to be philosophical about it. If a child is very sensitive to criticism or really insecure, then this isn't the business for them. You have to realise that you *are* going to get rejections, and you're going to have to learn to deal with that. The kid who goes to five castings and doesn't get anything has to learn that he's just got to go to five more. The best thing to do is just to keep going. I went through a period where I was going to casting after casting, after casting, and not getting anything. And you still go because each new job is different and, well ... the next one you could get!'

The more castings you attend, the more chance you have of success. Rachel York says, 'Some mums say, "We went on a casting last week, and we didn't get it. And we went on one the week before, and we didn't get. I don't want to do it any more. I'm sick of it." Well, that's the worst mentality you can have. You have to go on as many castings as you can or as we can get you. It's all about hedging your bets. If you bet on ten horses, there's more likelihood of you getting a winner, than if you just bet on one.'

Donna Hearn, mother of models Rebecca and Charlotte recalls, 'I think Charlotte had a few castings and got a lot of work straight away, she did well right from the start. Rebecca was younger and she didn't get much at first, but she's seven now and she really has done a lot of stuff.'

Parents can be put off by the number of other children competing for a job. They may think their child's chances of ever succeeding are slim. But Rachel York knows from her own experience that someone has to come out as the winner, 'You get people who think, "Oh at the casting, there were so many people!" but I just say, "Look, when I was doing this, I would go to a casting, and there would be loads of people – hundreds of them – and I got the job." So you never know what's going to happen.'

A cautionary note
Photographer, Daniel Pangbourne, urges parents to be realistic and to be prepared for the worst, 'You can go through all the processes: the interviews, having your pictures taken, going into the model book, but no one can promise you work. A child might get nothing because their look is wrong for that moment, or that year. They've got to realise that might happen: *they might never get a job*. They have to be prepared for that psychologically. Especially if they have a child who thinks, "I'm a model. I'm in the model book." If they never get a job, that could be very disappointing. They have to deal with that.'

If your child doesn't get the part ...
From a parent's perspective, getting news of an audition and going along to it with their child may be a very important event in their life. You will be on tenterhooks whilst waiting for the result of this audition. Something which you will have to be prepared for, is the fact that you *won't* be told if you *don't* get the part. It will come as a shock to many parents, but when a child goes to a casting or an audition, the only child who will hear anything afterwards is the child who gets the job. The rest of the children will hear nothing.

Rachel York explains why, 'We get to know all the models and their parents and it is horrible when someone goes for a casting and they don't get it. But we simply don't have time to tell everyone. We might have several castings on the go, every day. On each casting, there might be 25 kids out on it. When we find out that one of them has got the job, we have to phone them, and take the time with them, telling them all the arrangements. We just can't call the other 24 who didn't get the job. Because with each of those courtesy calls, every single mother or father would come out with the inevitable, "Oh ... why didn't they get it? What did they do wrong?" And the point is, they normally haven't done anything wrong, so there's nothing to explain. But all that would take so long, we just don't have the time to cope with it. It is one of the things that we stress when we take people on our books. You won't be told if you *don't* get the job. You'll only be told if you *do* get the job. It's not that we don't care, we *do* care. But we simply can't do it for every single person that doesn't get the job.'

Don't show your disappointment if your child doesn't get the job

If your child doesn't get a job, try to stress that it isn't important. Never underestimate the effect on your child if you show your disappointment. Agent Janis Penn reminds parents, 'If the child is rejected you've got to tell them that it's not that important. You've got to try to cover up your own disappointment for the sake of the child. You should tell them that to get to that stage in the audition was great. That they were pipped at the post for that one.'

If you show your disappointment to your child you could make them feel responsible and put unreasonable pressure on them. The damage it does can manifest itself in different ways, as Janis Penn explains, 'We had one kid who went for about 15 auditions. He was great! *But* there was something going wrong, and he just wasn't getting any jobs. His mother finally said to me, "Do you think this is worth it? Do you think it's ever going to work. I'm just getting so fed up." So I asked her, "Are you telling *him* you're fed up?" She said, "Well, he probably knows I'm disappointed." So I reassured her. I said, "He *is* great, and once it clicks for him, he's going to be fine. But you mustn't let him know that you're fed up – it'll put too much pressure on him." Well, sure enough, the next audition, she just approached it as a lovely day out – no pressure. And that time, whatever the boy did, he did it right. He got the job, and he just worked solidly after that.'

David York remembers how his mother behaved, 'My mother was very supportive. She never showed any disappointment. I know there are some mothers who, when their child doesn't get a part, want to know, "Why? Why not? My kid's excellent. He's the best!" But most parents take it very well. The best thing is just to have a "Don't worry, better luck next time" attitude. Parents have to keep this in mind – don't put pressure on. Be supportive, and don't show disappointment.'

Never attach blame

When a child doesn't get a job, their first thought will be that they did something wrong. You should dispel that thought immediately. It won't be constructive, it will just make them nervous and apprehensive about the next audition. Never give them the impression that if only they had done something differently they would have got the job.

Models' mother, Donna Hearn says, 'Becky and Charlie have been very fortunate – they've really had a lot of work. But if they don't get a job, I think what's most important is to let them know that it's not down to anything they've done wrong. It's just because they're not what the company are looking for. They know what they're looking for even before you've got in there.'

David York says, 'All I knew was that I was going to a casting to get a job, and I wanted to do everything right – to do whatever I had to do – to get it. So at first, when I wasn't getting any jobs, I blamed myself. I thought I was doing something wrong. But my mother took the time to explain to me that some jobs you get because you're right for the job. Some jobs you don't get because you're not right for the job. She helped me to understand that I might have exactly the right kind of personality that they're looking for, but they're looking for someone who's blond. And even as a kid I could understand that there was nothing I could do about that if they wanted a blond kid, or a shorter kid, or a taller kid … whatever they want is what they want. And it wasn't my fault.'

Don't make it a competition

There will be many children at a casting or an audition. If you don't get the job, it might be tempting to ask what qualities the child had who won the part. It is not a good idea to focus on this or to be making constant comparisons. It's best for your child to continue to be themselves, rather than to try to be more like another child.

David York says, 'When I first started out, if I was thinking anything, I was thinking, "Do I have what it takes?" I wasn't aware of thinking, "Oh this kid's so much better than me," or "He's better looking," or "He's cuter," or "He's got more freckles." I just didn't think about these things. I'm not a competitive person, and I wasn't as a child. But other children were different – they wanted desperately to be the winner! To be the one! But for me it wasn't quite like that. I never felt I had to beat anyone. I was never encouraged to feel that way. It's not like a race or anything like that. I think that's a healthier attitude to have.'

Lesley Simpson speaks about her model daughter's attitude to the other children she meets who are going for the same jobs, 'When Tiffany goes to auditions, she'll say to me, "Did you ask if any of my friends are going?" They like to meet up at auditions, they're not in competition with one another. They swap Christmas cards, all that sort of thing. She's made some really good friends going to auditions.'

Don't make it a test

You should never give your children the impression that they are being tested at a casting or an audition. If they don't 'pass', they will feel that they have done something wrong. Try to see the day out as an end in itself.

Daniel Pangbourne gives this advice, 'Don't have too much riding on it. Don't get too disappointed if you don't get the job. Make it a fun day.' In addition, he makes the point, 'Also remember that parent and child get to spend some time together on this day out.'

Whether it is mother and child or father and child, the time spent together one-to-one is valuable for both of you, no matter what age the child is.

Always be realistic – not every story is a success story

Janis Penn says, 'There are so many reasons that a child might be chosen. It could be a matter of two inches in height, or the eye colour, or it could be that one of the directors, or clients, takes to a certain child because they look like their own child! It could be anything. It doesn't necessarily mean to say that the child hasn't got "it". It could just mean that in this particular instance another child had a little bit more of "it".'

You must be tough and resilient
Former child model David York, thinks these are very important qualities to develop, 'You have to be tough and you have to be confident and just keep going for it. You have to tell yourself that even though you didn't get the last job, it was with other people. The next lot of people haven't seen you. It's a new audition, you have a new chance there. Of course, sometimes you'll go to a casting and you'll recognise the casting director and he or she will feel as if they know you from somewhere. So you tell them that you went to them for a casting. But that doesn't mean you automatically won't get it. You have to bear in mind that this casting is for a different job – with different demands. Just because you've seen a casting director before and they didn't take you doesn't mean that you're tainted. Each job they're looking to cast is different. You've just got to go in there, fresh faced, bright eyed and don't let it put you off just because you've seen them before.'

Rachel York says, 'I think the best way to deal with it is to remember that the client is looking for just *one thing* and that time around you just didn't fit the bill. It didn't work out, but it might the next. And if it doesn't work next time, it might work the time after that. I know that when I was doing it I went on lots of castings before I got a job.'

Recognise that it is a fickle world
Just as fashions come and go, so the children whose faces fit the fashion of the moment come and go. Mother of a child model, Lesley Simpson, has no illusions, 'It's a very fickle profession. This month people might want long blond hair and blue eyes. But next month the demand might not be for kids like that. It really doesn't matter. At the end of the day, the people at the audition have already got a rough idea of what they're looking for. And if my daughter doesn't fit that, well, she doesn't fit it! It's not anything she's done wrong. Tiffany went to one audition and they told me she smiled too much, they needed her to be more severe and I thought, so my daughter smiles too much ... I'm not going to moan about that!'

CHAPTER SIX CHECKLIST

Five questions to ask before you go to an audition:
1. What is the date of the shoot?
2. What is the date, time and location of the audition?
3. What kind of job is it, and what type of child are they looking for?
4. What will be required of your child?
5. If it is a commercial, what is the product being advertised?

Ten points to remember when you go to an audition:
1. Don't bring extra adults or children along. Interviewers want to see one chaperone and one child only.
2. You and your child should go in to the room relaxed, smiling, and happy to be there. One tip is to be prepared with a little joke to tell your child, just before you enter the room.
3. Encourage your child to be confident, to express themselves freely and to let their personality shine through.
4. Keep stress to a minimum, your children will pick up on it. Don't make the audition seem important. Do everything you can to arrive in plenty of time.
5. Make sure that your baby is as clean as possible from top to toe.
6. Take clean clothes in case of accidents.
7. Children should have *no* make-up and *no* jewellery on.
8. Don't place too much importance on 'training' or rehearsed audition pieces. Most people want a natural performance. They're looking for potential.
9. Don't be disappointed if you don't get the job, and never show any disappointment to your child.
10. Stay focused and enthusiastic. Keep going to castings even if you're not getting the work at first.

Seven things to remember if you don't get the part ...
1. Don't show your disappointment if your child doesn't get the job.
2. Never attach blame. Don't let your child think they did something wrong.
3. Don't make it seem like a competition by comparing your child to the child who won the part.
4. Don't make it seem like a test, by talking about 'passing' or 'failing'. Keep it fun.
5. Always be realistic – not every story is a success story.
6. Be tough and resilient and ready to try again.
7. Recognise that it is a fickle world.

CHAPTER SEVEN
There's No Business Like Show Business
Getting a job

You've got your first job, now what happens?

You and your child have been to the audition. It went well. Now you get a phone call informing you that your child has got the job. You're thrilled, you're excited and then, as it sinks in, you begin to feel nervous. Your child will be looking to you for guidance, information and reassurance. Children expect parents to have the answers to everything, but you realise you aren't sure what to expect.

The worst thing you can do

Of course, it was a great achievement that your child got through the casting or audition to be chosen, and naturally you feel your child is special, but don't expect 'star' treatment. No matter how exciting an event this first job is for you and your family, remember that it's a regular day at work for the people you are going to meet. Your child is about to enter a professional environment and will be expected to have a professional attitude. Never go to a job expecting the people around you to be able to take time away from their work to explain everything that is happening and everything that is expected of you. Remember that each person on a set has their own responsibilities: be sensitive to the pressure they are under to get their own job done. People will normally be friendly and willing to help you as long as you choose the right moment to ask them.

The best thing you can do

Learn as much as you can about the workplace which you will be entering and the part your child will play in it. Find out not only about the job your child will be doing, but also about the jobs the people around you will be doing. Learn about the etiquette of the workplace. Getting a job is one thing, but getting a good reputation and being asked back to do more work will be dependent on how well your child does.

The first thing to do
Between the casting and the shoot ... do nothing! Stay the same.

Don't change a thing
Your child has been cast on the basis of the way they looked at the audition. Don't go and get your child's hair cut (or permed, or change its colour!) in between the casting, or the audition, and the shoot. If a child turns up at the shoot after they've had a haircut *everyone* will be upset.

Trying to keep everything the same for the shoot as it was at the casting can also mean keeping things *around* a child the same. Baby wrangler, Cat Sulley says, 'If mum brings a baby to the casting and then it's dad who brings the baby to the job, it can cause problems. Sometimes babies can be a lot more clingy to their dads.' Be aware of the fact that your child might behave differently depending on whom they are with. The best plan is that whoever takes the child to the casting, is the person to go with the child for the shoot.

The Shoot
This section will provide you with a detailed description of three different work situations:
1. Working on a Photographic Shoot
2. Working on Live TV
3. Working on a Film or Television Set for Drama or commercials

There is a glossary at the end of this chapter with a list of the job titles that people have and a description of the jobs they do. You will also find explanations of expressions and terms which you are likely to encounter on a shoot.

But first, here is some general advice which applies to every job.

Facts to find out from your agent as soon as you are told about the job

Ask your agent for the following information, and keep a note of the details safe in a plastic pocket in your ring binder.

Name of company and name of contact person

You need to know exactly who is employing your child, if it is a photographer doing an advertising shoot for a product, take a note of the photographer's client, too. If it is a film or television shoot, get the name of the production company and the name of the production. Also get the name of the contact person whom you should ask for when you arrive. Ascertain their position, too, e.g. **P.A.** (production assistant), **A.D.** (assistant director), **stage manager**, etc. (see the glossary at the end of this chapter for an explanation of jobs).

Description of your child's job

Always ask in advance what your child will be expected to do, so that they can prepare beforehand, if necessary. Get the most up-to-date information about the regulations governing the working conditions of your child. Agent Janis Penn says, 'There are strict limits, constantly changing rules and laws for different situations. Parents should check with us before each job. We'll be able to tell them all about the work hours and rest hours.'

Wardrobe and props

Ask if you have to provide anything, what items of clothing your child should wear, or what **props** you should take along (e.g. rollerskates or skateboards). If you have to provide your child's own clothes, ask what exactly is expected. Janis Penn says, 'We normally advise parents to take along a choice of items to wear, unless it's a clothing company in which case they're modelling clothes which are provided. Never take anything with logos – don't advertise any other products on your clothes – just take plain, coloured tops.

Make-up and hair

Find out if a make-up artist will be in attendance, or if you will be expected to do your child's own hair. If you have to do it, be clear about exactly what they are expecting.

Address of location

Take an accurate note of the location and a contact telephone number in case you have any problems getting there.

Transport

Ask if any transportation will be provided. If you are working on a film, there may be a pick-up point for you to meet a bus which will take you to the location. Make sure that you arrive at the appropriate place in good time.

Dates and times

Double check the date or dates for which you are booked. Pay particular attention to the final date when you will be required. Remember that for the sake of **continuity** your child has to look the same at the end as they did at the beginning, so cancel any hairdresser's appointments. Get an estimate of how long you will be expected to be there. Photo shoots may be as little as one or two hours. Film or television shoots can require you to be in attendance and on call all day. If you have to arrange a baby sitter for other children at home, be sure to allow extra time in case you are delayed.

Refreshments

Ask what will be provided in terms of snacks, drinks, lunch etc. It's important to know if you need to bring along anything yourself for you and your child.

Fee

Take a note of the fee your child will be expecting for this job. (See the section on *Looking after the finances* in Chapter Eight).

Going to the job
Get there, and get there on time
Needless to say, if you do commit yourself to a job you must turn up!
Failing to show up for work causes everyone problems. Being unreliable
will damage your reputation and result in you not being put forward for
any other jobs.

Agent, Janis Penn says, 'Recently, one mother simply didn't turn up for
a job and didn't even bother to call us. It really threw everything out
because it was for a triple shot – that's one with three children – we had
a last minute panic trying to find another child to fit the bill. We had to
phone another agent as we didn't have a child who was right for the role.
The client had to pay for everyone – all the other models and chaperones
– to wait for another hour on top of what they were expecting to pay. So
the whole thing was a real nightmare.'

Opera and theatre director, Robert Jones, has a warning for parents
who don't take their commitment seriously, 'At pantomime time children
are always in demand. One mother of two ebullient daughters had
managed to get both girls into the same production of "Hansel and
Gretel". However, during the run of the show, these apparently robust
children both suffered from mysterious, though short-lived, viral
ailments. The diagnosis was confirmed when one of our company
management visited another show in town one night and saw both girls'
names on the programme. On making discreet enquiries she found that
both girls had enjoyed the same ill health during their run as during ours.
The unfortunate children were sacked from both shows and, quite literally,
never worked in that town again.'

No one will hold it against you if you have a genuine emergency and
are suddenly unable to attend a job. Make sure that you telephone your
agent and inform them as soon as you possibly can.

When you arrive
Check in
The first thing to do when you get to the location of the shoot, is to let

someone know that you have arrived. If you are at a studio, you will introduce yourself at reception, and someone will come to collect you. If you are at another location, ask someone if they can tell you where to find the contact person (you'll have their name and job title in your notes). Check in with them, and take this opportunity to ask a few questions. You are less likely to do the wrong thing on a shoot if you have all the facts. Don't be afraid to ask for clarification about things when you arrive, but make sure you have paper and pen ready to take notes. People will be happy to answer your questions, especially at the start of the day, but it's not a good idea to keep returning to them and asking the same question more than once.

Names of key personnel

Find out the names of the people your will be interacting with:

On a photographic shoot:
The photographer
Photographer's assistant
The stylist
The baby wrangler

On a TV or film shoot:
The director
The A.D. (assistant director, floor manager)
The P.A. (production assistant)
Wardrobe
Make-up
(Read the section at the end of this chapter explaining the jobs all the various people do, then if you have a question to ask, you will be able to direct it to the correct person.)

Toilet facilities

Find out where toilets and washrooms are located. It's essential that you and your child are comfortable at all times. Ask where the facilities are when you arrive, this will save you from having to ask later when people are busy doing other things and the situation is becoming urgent for you or your child!

Refreshment facilities

Ask what refreshments will be provided, what times they will be available, and where they can be obtained. If you are clear about what you are entitled to, and where and when you can get access to it, then you won't feel uncomfortable asking for it when you need it.

Points to remember when working on a shoot
Professional behaviour

Professional behaviour is expected at all times. Always bear in mind that your child is doing a job. When you are there looking after them, you are being employed as a chaperone. There will be more likelihood that you will be asked to work again if you impress people with your professionalism. Casting director, Suzy Korel, says, 'Parents have to understand that it is their job, on a shoot, to look after their kids and they're being paid accordingly. I've had phone calls from clients saying the mother was getting in everybody's way and that all she was interested in was her food. They have to remember they're not being paid to come along and have free food, they're there to look after their kids.'

The chaperone

One child, one chaperone is the rule unless you have more than one child working on a shoot, never take other children along. You should also never invite other adults along to a shoot.

Baby wrangler, Cat Sulley, says, 'Sometimes we get both parents coming along, but we prefer just one. We've also had mum, dad, and grandparents. I understand that it's exciting when your child gets a job, but we can't cope with that number of people when we're trying to work. The photographer has a difficult job to do. So just remember that you're putting your child forward for a job, and that's what they're supposed to be doing. It's not a family day outing to see your daughter have her photograph taken. Bringing along brothers and sisters, too, is a problem. Mums often find it difficult to cope with kids who get bored: and they do get bored, especially if they are not involved in the shoot.'

Film and television sets are formal and 'closed' to anyone not directly involved with the shoot. Anyone who doesn't have specific permission to be there, will simply be asked to remove themselves from the set by the A.D. or floor manager.

Know your child's rights

You should know the agreements and regulations relating to your child in the workplace, according to the type of work they will be doing. Your agent will always be able to advise you on the different laws governing the various environments. It is then up to you to speak up on your child's behalf if any of these regulations are being breached. You are there in the professional capacity of chaperone.

Diana Bell, a professional chaperone, says, 'The chaperone, in many cases, actually has more power than the director or producer, as it is the chaperone's job to ensure that the strict rules are enforced as to the length of time a child spends on set, on stage, or rehearsing etc. This can literally mean stepping in and stopping a vital take because the child is due a ten minute break. This takes serious guts and an air of authority.'

Know your child's place

At the same time as you are protecting your child and standing up for their rights, you must also be discreet and try not to get in the way of the production. Be sensitive to the fact that everyone else on the shoot has a job to do and that they will have priorities. Your child, especially if they are being employed as an extra for background work, is a very small cog in the context of the whole machine.

Rules on set

Whether on a television or film set or in a photographer's studio, the most difficult thing for parents and children to cope with is the requirement to keep quiet while everyone else is working.

Baby wrangler, Cat Sulley explains, 'Very often parents just don't understand that when a photographer is shooting, he's trying to concentrate. It's an incredibly difficult job to do. And if you've got people nattering away in the background, it can be very distracting, not only for the photographer but for the child he's trying to shoot, as well.'

If you are the mother of a young baby, you may want to become involved with child modelling as a way to get yourself out of the house. Perhaps having a young baby has left you feeling trapped and isolated. Getting out and about is a very healthy thing for both mother and child, and offers you the chance to meet people. It's natural that you will want to chat to people in your spare moments, but when people are working, you will often have to remain silent. Diana Bell speaks about being a chaperone in a theatre, 'Large chorus-size dressing rooms in council run theatres are often situated right under the stage so everyone has to be totally silent. Chaperoning child performers in a theatre means knowing the running order of the show inside out, ferrying the right child(ren) from dressing room to wings as required, all in *total silence*. You also need to know a whole wealth of silent finger plays, card games, and tricks to stop the giggles.'

Boredom
Be prepared for boredom and take things along to keep your child occupied. There may be long periods, especially if you are working in television or film, where you will be doing nothing but waiting to be called. You will have to keep your children entertained. Take along books, paper, pencils, anything that will provide silent entertainment.

Former child model, David York, now working in a model agency says, 'Filming for a commercial you're going to be sitting around for eight hours out of the day and shooting for one. Eventually you think, "Okay, I'm going to be stuck in this room, hanging around all day, I'm going to get really bored." So it helps to *be prepared for boredom*. I remember one job where I was kept waiting all day and at the end of the day they came along to me and said, "Actually we won't be needing you today." I'd read everything I'd brought with me, twice over. I'd exhausted everything. And

I just kept thinking about all the other things I could have been doing. It seemed like such a waste of time! I still got paid, but it was *so* boring.'

You are being paid for the hours of waiting as well as the hours of performing, so you have to accept that it is all part of the job. If you are prepared in advance, you can make sure that the time is spent productively. David advises, 'Bring books to read. Or homework to do. We get complaints from parents who say, "We sat around for four hours!" and we have to try to explain to them that that's the way it is. You have to accept that. You have to keep yourself occupied.'

Donna Hearn, mother of model daughters, says, 'The first time we went along, I didn't have anything. But it's just common sense really. Just take things along. You know they're going to get bored even if they're only hanging about for five minutes. Even if they're *doing* something, they're going to get bored doing it! So I just take things like a bag with paper and colouring pens. Becky's just started tapestry, so that's ideal, and Becky and Charlie are such little professionals they'll even go over to the other children, and say, "Do you want to draw?" or "Do you want to play *I spy*?" They're so good about it. They take it in their stride because they've done a lot of work. They're both really confident and if there's a child around that's not so confident, they'll try to get that child to relax and try to get them to join in.'

Television director, Fiona Cumming, recalls, 'The nicest family that I ever worked with was one in which all four children were involved in the acting business. I worked at different times with each of them and on one occasion all four were in the same drama. But no matter how many were there, the moment they arrived on location, Mum would take them to a table and open a large "activity bag" which contained everything required to keep them quiet and occupied during the day – even the tiniest child had his own drawing "project"! They were never bored, always alert, very down-to-earth and not at all precocious ... an absolute joy to work with.'

It will be difficult, but you will have to try to keep your child alert. The danger is that if your child gets bored, they will lose their focus and enthusiasm. They will need all their energy when they are required **on set**, so it's best if you can find some way of preventing them from getting too bored and lethargic.

Baby wrangler, Cat Sulley, says, 'Parents know how to look after their kids, but they don't always know how to keep them amused, without being over-excited, when they're not being photographed. During a four or five hour session there might be different **set ups**, with different lighting and I look after the children when they're not being used on the shoot, as well as when they are. A lot of the time when you're working with three or four year-olds their energy will last a lot longer than older kids. So we'll sit together, playing word association games or maybe they'll have some homework to work on, and that keeps them alert, but I try to save their energy for the actual shoot.'

Energy

At the other end of the scale, occasionally too much energy can be a problem! Be careful about what your child eats on set. When refreshments are available on a film or television shoot you will find that location caterers often provide a selection of sweet snacks and drinks. These are appreciated by adults who are working long hours and need to keep their energy levels up. The sight of these will be very tempting for any child, but try to avoid chocolate or drinks filled with sugar as they have the effect of charging up your child with energy, and that can have an unpredictable outcome. Everyone has to be able to work with your child: that means keeping them in a balanced and manageable state of mind.

Opera and theatre director, Robert Jones, says 'Children often find a large rehearsal room full of props a great temptation to go wild. I was working once with a boy who was terrifyingly energetic, and I thought I'd better have a word with his parents during the tea break. I popped into the canteen to find the boy tucking into a large helping of chocolate cake and washing it down with a fizzy drink. From that moment I started to ask parents not to feed their children sweets, crisps, coloured cheese, or anything with orange colouring in it on the days when they are working. Now I don't have to scrape the kids off the ceiling, and the parents tell me that the children sleep better at night.'

Food and drink

Still on the subject of food and drink. Keep all food and drink well away from the set, and don't allow your child to wander around while eating or drinking. If they are between **takes** and their outfit is being used on the shoot, take special care to avoid spillages on your child's clothes, especially if has been provided by the wardrobe department, or is a specially made sample of clothes for a fashion company's launch!

Instructions

Always listen carefully and take a note of what you are told. Make sure that you are clear, especially about what you have to do, where you have to be and when you have to be there. Comply with these instructions. Ask for clarification at the time you are being told, if you need it. Never suffer the discomfort or anxiety of sitting, not knowing what is going on or what you are supposed to do.

Props

Don't touch or remove anything from the set. Everything which is on a set has been placed there for a purpose: you and your child must respect this. Never move or remove any prop no matter how large or small.

Clothes, hair and make-up

Once your child's wardrobe, hair and make-up has been approved, never alter it. It's vital that you keep it the same for continuity. If your child is in discomfort and needs to change something, get approval first.

Breaks

If you need to take a break or to take your child to the toilet, be sure to let someone know, in case your child is suddenly required on set. Tell the photographer's assistant, the P.A. or the A.D. where you are going and be sure to return as soon as you can.

A tip for babies

If you have a young baby bring a favourite toy which makes them smile.

Keep it hidden away in a bag, but have it handy and be ready to bring it out if required.

Pack a bag
Pack a bag to cope with all your needs. Don't forget the following items:
- All the information (in plastic pockets) which you need about the shoot
- Spare plastic pockets for receipts
- Paper and pen for taking notes
- Clean underwear or changing kit for baby (with sufficient changes for the day)
- Baby wipes
- Tissues
- Sun protection cream (with a high protection factor) if working outdoors
- Simple change of clothes in case of spills
- Books, paper and pencils, activity pack or favourite toy for baby
- Make-up cover stick for any blemishes
- Hairbrush, comb, clasps or hairbands
- Healthy snacks or drinks (without sugar)
- Repair Kit: safety pins, needle and thread
- First Aid Kit: antiseptic wipes and sticking plasters in case of scrapes
- Any medications your child might require

Valuables
Don't bring any unnecessary valuables to a shoot. Your attention will be on your child, and it could be easy for belongings to get lost or be stolen. Remove any jewellery your child wears, e.g. earrings, before setting off for the shoot, and leave it safely at home.

Background and extra work
All of the above advice applies equally to children employed as extras on television or film, however, there are some additional considerations for the child who is employed as an extra.

Keep a low profile. Your child is being employed to be in the background. People will appreciate it if you stay in the background both while you are working and while you are not working. Don't expect special attention and try not to get in the way.

Catering. Look out for special arrangements for extras or background artistes. If there isn't a separate catering wagon, or table, then you should always hang back and go last, don't got to the start of the queue. Crew and featured artistes should be allowed to go first.

Problems on set
Be calm when dealing with problems on set. If a disagreement or conflict arises, deal with it quietly and calmly. Remove your child from earshot and keep them out of the discussion. State your position rationally and listen carefully to the other person's point of view. If it is not possible to resolve the matter to your satisfaction, it may be necessary telephone your agent. Respect your agent's advice. If they take the matter in hand, accept their word on the final resolution. Above all, try not to hold up the shoot as this will create additional tension.

Don't forget anything
Other people on the shoot won't be able to remember which items belong to whom. If you forget any of your or your child's belongings, they may be kept for a certain length of time, but they won't be kept forever: therefore you may not see them again. Make sure you gather up all of your belongings and take them with you when you leave.

Check out
At the end of the working day, confirm how many hours you and your child have been there, and make sure that you have clearance to leave. Ask if you will be required again, and if so, confirm the date and time. Take notes of all of these details and keep them in your folder.

Confidentiality

Your child is involved in creating images which will not be available to the general public for some time, perhaps months. You will have access to privileged information and you must treat it confidentially. Whether it is a new fashion line or the dramatic denouement of a television series or a film, the client or producers will want sole control over when and how the information is released. It is important that you and your child can keep a secret and take this responsibility seriously.

Finally ... report back to your agent

When you get home, contact your agent and let them know exactly how the job went. Your agent needs to know how many hours you worked. In addition, you should let your agent know if anything unexpected happened on the shoot. You should tell your agent if you felt something went wrong, or if you had any disagreements or trouble with anyone on the shoot.

Working on a photographic shoot

Every shoot is different, depending on the product and the age of the children involved. A baby shoot will be totally different from a shoot involving nine year-olds. The photographer will have a different way of communicating and a different way of motivating the children.

Don't forget – one child one chaperone. It is easy to imagine that a photographic session is going to be similar to a family portrait session: that the photographer is just going to set up your child and take a picture, and that you can take the family along to watch. Photographer, Daniel Pangbourne, implores, 'When you turn up ... please don't turn up with ten people! One time, we had mum, dad, grandparents, the other two kids ... and the family labrador! They all walked in! I had to say, "I'm sorry, only one person can accompany the child." And they were all really upset, because they'd all travelled miles to be here. They said, "But we've come to see our child's first shoot." I had to say I was sorry, I didn't want to disappoint them, but we just couldn't cope with all of them in the studio. And we don't have dogs in the studio, ever! Generally parents are really nice, and parents are really important to the whole shoot. But most agencies will specify: *one parent, one child*. It's all we can cope with in a studio, when we're working.'

What you have to be aware of, is that there is a commercial aspect to your child having been chosen. Your child has the 'look' which a client wants, but it's not simply a picture of your child, the client is looking for. The child is only one part of the image, and may not be the only model involved. The most important thing in the picture is the client's *product*. The photographer is trying to capture an image which does several things: it has to be eye-catching, appealing, well-composed, and make the product look like something which people will want to buy. Parents should realise that the photographer is under pressure of time to take photographs with which the client will be happy. It is complex and demanding; it means juggling a lot of factors – not least of all, unpredictable children – and requires a lot of concentration. For that reason, it will be appreciated if you do everything you can to make the photographer's job smoother. Abiding by the rule of 'one child, one chaperone' is the best start you can make.

Bear in mind that your child might not be used
Parents have to realise that their child might not be used. For every one child a photographer needs, they will have at least one more standing by. You might turn up to discover that three four year-olds have been called to do a shot, but only one of them gets used. Be prepared for the fact that your child's face might not end up in the catalogue or in the magazine or on the packaging. It might be disappointing to you and your child not to be used after having succeeded in getting through the casting but you will still be paid for turning up. In the case of babies, photographers will have a minimum of three for every one they need. So if they are shooting five babies in a day, they will call 15 or 20 babies to the studio. Babies and toddlers can be very unpredictable. No one can ask a baby to do anything. Photographers have to hope to catch the right look, at the right moment. If a baby can manage not to cry it's a start and if they've got half a smile, it's a bonus. But in the event that a child won't stop crying, the photographer will have to move on to one of the back-up children. That

way, the photographer can be confident about getting the shots required. Photographers have to hedge their bets. With a large crew standing by to work, they can't risk not getting the shots that they need. They always have to have back-ups.

Daniel Pangbourne says, 'A lot of parents get stressed if the kids won't do what's required. But no one holds the parents or the kids responsible for that; especially with toddlers, two and three year-olds, we've had them turn up and decide they're not going on set. They just want to go home. It does happen now and then. And I think that's more embarrassing and stressful for the parents than anything. But that's why we have a back-up child.'

If your child refuses, point blank, to go on set, then there is a chance that they might not get paid. However, if they go on set and they're simply not very good – as long as they are willing to walk on and get their picture taken – they will be paid. But you should never try and force them to do it. That's why it's essential to establish from the outset that this is something your child wants to do.

A *photographer's schedule*
In general, models don't have a lot of waiting time in photographer's studios. Models are paid by the hour for their time, so the schedule is usually quite tight. For this reason, it's important that you don't arrive late. If you don't turn up on time, the photographer will have to move on to the next model and you will miss your slot altogether. It is simply not possible to hold up everyone and delay a whole day's shooting because one model is late.

If your call is at 4pm, and you arrive at 3.59pm – then you will have to get straight into the job. There will be no time to spare. This won't give your child time to relax and become accustomed to the studio. The ideal approach is to arrive a little bit early – about a quarter of an hour or 20 minutes – then you will probably be offered a cup of tea or coffee. You will have time to relax and get comfortable. You'll have plenty of time to take your child to the toilet and freshen up before they start their job. It's better to turn up too early and to walk around the block, than to be late.

The procedure

The detail of every job will be different. But the normal procedure will be that when you arrive you will be offered tea or coffee and asked to sit down and wait until you are called. The **stylist**, the **client** or the photographer will introduce themselves to you and then they will explain what they will be doing that day. They will probably show you a **layout**, and tell you what you can expect to have to do. First your child will have their hair and make-up attended to, then the stylist will select the clothes they'll be wearing, and get them ready. After that, your child will be asked on to **the set** and the photographer will take the pictures.

Photographer, Daniel Pangbourne, says that in the ideal situation, everything is communicated to the parent, but he admits that sometimes people take it for granted that the parent will know what the form is, 'If they are new to it, and they don't know what to expect, then the parent and child can be sitting there, petrified. They don't know what's happening next or what they should be doing. I think a lot of it is just about relaxing, and waiting ... or asking!'

Don't be afraid to speak up if you feel uncomfortable or aren't sure what is going on. Without becoming a nuisance, it's reasonable for you to ask things such as:

■ Where would you like us to wait?
■ Can you tell us how long will we be here?
■ What are we going to be doing?
■ Who is the photographer?
■ Who is the stylist?

Daniel Pangbourne says, 'But if you don't know what a stylist is, or what they do, then you don't know why you'd be asking who the stylist is! The average person on the street has no idea what a stylist does.'

Some things you will learn by experience, others you can learn by doing research beforehand. The glossary at the end of this chapter will provide you with a short-cut to becoming familiar with the expressions and terms used on a shoot as well as job descriptions of the people you will meet.

Still photography is very much more low-key than TV or film. There are fewer people involved in a photographic shoot. Parents coming in to this environment will generally meet a photographer and a stylist who work together. The stylist will look after the child's clothes and make-up. Sometimes there might be a separate hair and make-up artist. During the shoot, it's really down to the stylist and the photographer to encourage and cajole the children. They will speak to them and motivate them to get the sort of shots required. Sometimes a **baby wrangler** will be used. Often, the parents will be asked to help as well. Daniel Pangbourne says, 'If it's a baby shoot, I'll often use the parents as much as I can to help me to get the best out of the kids. A lot of the time, the parents know best how to motivate the kids.' The difficult part for the parent is knowing when to step back to let the photographer get on with his job. Daniel says, 'You want the parents to be supportive in what you're trying to do. But not to interfere. And that is a fine line. Some parents learn it very easily and some don't, unfortunately.'

Respect the photographer's position

The photographer has a clear image of the look that he is trying to capture. It is important that you don't offer unwanted opinions or try to interfere with the shoot. Daniel says, 'I have had parents saying things like, "My daughter doesn't like wearing blue" or, "My daughter should be wearing that outfit, not that one." This puts the everyone in an embarrassing situation. Remember that it's not your place to choose the clothes or comment upon how your child should look.'

Protect your child

Of course it is a different matter if you feel that the photographs are in some way inappropriate, or if you feel you child is being asked to do something of which you disapprove. In this situation, you would have the right to step in immediately and remove your child from the set and the premises. You should also report the matter immediately to your agent.

Never take pictures or video

It is forbidden for you to take your own pictures or video on set. There are good reasons for this.

Product confidentiality. Competition and launch dates for products are crucial. A lot of photographic work is done months or even a year in advance and the amount of research that is put into a product amounts to vast sums of money, so for a rival to get to know something about a product before it's released can be very important to the manufacturers. Photographers are required to sign a confidentiality clause to say that they won't tell anyone about the product. If these products are on view, on the set, you can understand why no-one is allowed to take pictures on the set which might include an image of the product. An obvious example would be of a range of fashion clothes which no one is allowed to view for another six months until they are released.

Damage to equipment. Another reason that photographs are not allowed on set is that if a flash goes off it can activate all the other flashes which are set up in the studio. These professional flashes have a specific recycle time. If they flash once again before their proper recycle time, it can blow the pack and ruin it. In this situation, thousands of pounds worth of equipment can be at stake.

When the photographer is shooting, always keep quiet

Remember that voices carry easily in a studio environment. If you are waiting **off set** while the photographer is working, you should be as quiet as possible. The photographer is trying hard to get the right shot and the children with whom he is working could easily be distracted. Remember that this particular job could be crucial to the photographer's livelihood, his reputation, his career. A great photograph is taken in a fraction of a second and a vital moment could be lost forever if the concentration **on set** is broken by chatter, giggling, or other noises off set.

Working on live TV

Magazine programmes or daytime chat shows often bring children in to animate a feature which they are covering. Your child might be asked to model a range of children's clothes, to try out a range of new toys, or to participate in something seasonal, such as a manger scene at Christmas time. Donna Hearn's daughter Becky was invited on to a programme at

Hallowe'en, 'She had to go on as a pumpkin, and then she went back the following year as something else. She's been invited back loads of times.'

Live TV changes by the minute – you may not be used

Once again, the possibility that you will not be used should be the first thing that you consider. Live television is constantly changing and moving on. News and current affairs items may be picked up and dropped at a moment's notice.

Charles Moritz speaks of one experience whilst working as a **researcher** for Granada Television, 'I was asked to arrange for a load of mothers and babies to appear live in studio for a news item. I went to all kinds of trouble to get the mums in question to go to all kinds of trouble to get there and be ready ... and then the producer suddenly changed his mind and stood the item down.'

Don't get your hopes up, or get too excited about the prospect of friends and family seeing your child on television, it may come to nothing at the end of the day. You will have to accept this as a risk. Protect yourself by ensuring that a fee is agreed to compensate you whether or not the item goes ahead.

The procedure in a television studio

The labyrinthine nature of most television studios means that you will be met at reception and accompanied at all times so that you don't get lost. You will be met by a researcher, or **assistant stage manager** and will normally be taken first to the **green room**, or canteen where you will be offered tea, coffee, or the chance to freshen up.

You will then be taken to **wardrobe** and **make-up**, and depending on what your child is being asked to do, they will be dressed and made up. Once your child is ready to go on, you'll be taken back to the green room until you receive your **call**. Live television is normally kept to a tight schedule.

You will enter the **studio** through a large sound-proofed door. A red light will be flashing outside all the time while the cameras are **on-air**, or **recording**. You will probably be allowed to accompany your child into the studio: if you are, then take care not to stray on set, and to be very quiet. You must not get in the way of the cameras or their cables as they glide across the floor on large pedestals; and be aware that any sound that you make could be picked up by the microphones.

The first time you encounter a studio environment it will seem very strange. There is a lot of large equipment, cameras, lights; the set is very brightly lit, and everything off set is gloomy and dark by comparison. It is easy to be overawed. You should try to be as relaxed as possible about it. A child has few preconceptions and will readily accept things if you encourage them. Oddly, you may discover that your child adapts to it all even more quickly than you.

Television producer and director, Martyn Day, describes his experience of working with a young child in a show called 'Our Backyard' which was recorded in a television studio, 'The strange thing was the 4 year-old child, Laura. Without any stage training or rehearsal Laura took to the situation completely naturally. She really believed that the studio "house" was a real house and the "backyard" a backyard, and the fact that it was all inside a studio didn't disturb her at all. Even the lumbering studio pedestal cameras she dismissed as "big vacuum cleaners". On one occasion in a programme set at night time, when the actors built a barbecue "under the stars" and sang lullabies to Laura, she obliged us all by gently falling asleep! Children can constantly surprise us. Their imagination is endless and their ability to suspend disbelief complete. Laura made it real, because she wanted it to be real and so, in her mind at least, it was.'

Lesley Simpson discovered that her daughter's idea of what was going on in a television studio was quite different from the truth. She says, 'At school, Tiffany was asked to sing a solo and read in front of the assembly and she got a bit shy about it. Her teacher couldn't understand how she could be shy when she'd done so much stuff on television. And Tiffany said, "But there weren't many people watching." As far as she was concerned, the only people there, were the ones she could see in the studio. She had no idea how many people were watching her on TV!'

For your child to make the best impression you want them to be as relaxed and happy as possible. Even if you are very excited about the prospect of millions of people seeing your child, it's best for the child if you don't stress this to them.

Tiffany's innocence certainly seems to help her to take the bright lights in her stride, her mother Lesley remembers one occasion in particular, 'Tiffany was on a TV show and Janet Jackson was on the same show. Afterwards she asked Tiffany, "Would you like your photograph taken with me?" and Tiffany replied very politely, "No thank you." And I said, "Go on Tiffany have your picture taken." The truth was, I wanted to have *my* picture taken with Janet Jackson – I think she's great! But Tiffany still said very coolly, "No thank you I don't want one." We still laugh about that now.'

Of course, some children take to performing like ducks to water, and may surprise you by demonstrating that they know *exactly* what is required even at the earliest age. Donna Hearn remembers watching her daughter doing a live daytime magazine programme, 'Becky was a fairy and the presenters were chatting to the children, and one of them asked her, "And how old are you, Rebecca?" And Becky put on the cutest little baby voice and whispered, "I'm five ... but in eight more sleeps I'm going to be six." She had them wrapped round her little finger. They were so charmed by her she's been asked back on several times since then.'

Once your child has made their appearance you will be taken back to wardrobe and make-up to return any clothes and to get cleaned up, after which you will be accompanied to the exit.

Working on a film or television set for drama or commercials

The first thing to check in the contract and **schedule** for a part in a film or television drama are your start and finish dates. The **shoot** may take place over a number of weeks, even months, and it's absolutely essential for reasons of **continuity** that a performer's appearance remains exactly the same during that time. Long hair must not be cut short. The make-up department can work wonders, but they won't appreciate having to track down a wig an hour before a performer is due on set. Any activities which could result in broken limbs, such as ice skating or skiing, should be avoided.

Television producer, Peter May recalls, 'In the middle of a long and big budget shoot, a company arrived nearby and set up a "Bungee Jump". I couldn't believe it when I discovered that a number of the actors had booked themselves on it to have a go! Of course you're perfectly free to put life and limb at risk, but remember that when you're under contract for the duration of a shoot, you have a responsibility to the production to take care of yourself.' Not even the most creative wardrobe department can manage to hide crutches and a plaster cast. So take special care for the duration of the contract. The first responsibility of a performer is to turn up each day on set looking the way the **director** expects.

A television or film set is like a huge engine. All the individual parts of it have their own important function and all the people are like cogs and wheels, interconnected and dependent on one another. It's vital to know where you fit into the machinery and exactly what is expected. Once a production is underway, everyone will be so busy with their own responsibilities that no one will have time to explain anything to the novice. Professionals in the television and film industry take their jobs very seriously because when that big engine starts up, everyone has to be in their place, doing their job, at the right moment. If someone gets something wrong, everything grinds to a halt and it's immediately apparent to the entire cast and crew who is to blame. As a result of this, stress levels are high. Be sensitive to the fact that the people involved in a shoot for a movie or large scale television drama are all under pressure.

The schedule
The greatest pressure of all is to keep to the schedule. Taking an extra half an hour to finish a morning's work may not seem like much, but carrying on at that pace means an extra hour per day, and over a 40 or 50 day shoot that adds up to an extra week on the schedule. To a **producer** that means that the budget will run over by ten of thousands of pounds. The phrase 'time is money' is no cliché in this area of the business.

The procedure
Child performers, whether they have a **featured part** or they are **extras**, will

find that their point of contact with the production will be the **3rd assistant director** (or '**Third**') in a film, or the **stage manager** in a television studio drama. This is the person who will telephone to make arrangements and who will post or hand out the schedules and **call sheets** which show your **call time**, or the time that you will be expected to arrive on the day of the shoot.

It goes without saying therefore that a performer – even a humble non-speaking extra – must never be late. But don't be surprised to receive an instruction to be at the wardrobe department at 6am, then not to be called on set until 10.30am.

The thing which strikes everyone on their first visit to a film or television set is the amount of time which people spend *waiting around*. Everyone has to wait for their turn to make their contribution and the performers have to wait longer than anyone else. Being patient, and taking something along to fill in the time will help stop boredom setting in. Remember that when called on set the performer is expected to be word and performance perfect and full of energy. Anyone who has been sitting doing nothing for four hours will quickly become fed up and jaded, but children and young people will suffer this even more acutely.

It helps to understand what the processes are, which take up so much time.

The working day

The earliest risers are the wardrobe and make-up departments. They will start preparing sometimes as early as 4am, to dress the cast and fix the performers' hair and make-up. Every performer will be given an appointment with both of these departments at the start of their day's work. There is a limit to the number of assistants employed, so on a large shoot the schedule of appointments can start very early in the morning in order that everyone can be given the individual attention they require. Punctuality is imperative here. The appointments may be as little as ten or fifteen minutes apart and anyone who turns up even a few minutes late will throw the schedule out for wardrobe and make-up for the rest of the day.

While the performers are getting dressed and made up, everyone else is getting the set ready for the first scene of the day. The **designer** and **stage hands** are preparing the **set** and **props**, the **gaffer** and electricians are laying cables and setting up the lights, the director will be discussing the shots he wants with his camera operator. The **1st A.D.** or **floor manager** will be keeping tabs on everyone, making sure that everything is running to schedule, and that there are no problems. During this time caterers will normally provide breakfast, tea, coffee, and soft drinks. All performers have to take extra care to protect their costumes from accidental spillages!

After breakfast, the waiting begins.

A single **scene** in a drama may consist of only two or three pages of dialogue in the **script**, but the director splits this up and makes a plan of exactly how he wants the audience to see it so he divides it into many different shots. He may want to view every line of script from a different angle. If two actors are talking in a scene, he may want a **close-up** of one actor's face, and then the **reverse** close-up of the other actor's face. He may want shots of the actors walking, moving, getting into a car – and each of these shots will require a separate set-up.

When finally called on set the performers will normally perform a **walk-through** of the scene simply to allow the camera and **boom operator** to see the moves which will be made. Next, there will be a **rehearsal** of the scene with full performances. Finally, there will be a **take**. Even if the first take is perfect, the director will ask for it to be done again so that he has two copies of it in case of any technical problems. Normally there will be numerous takes, as it is rare for everyone to deliver their best performance at the same time with no technical hitches. When going for another take, the 1st assistant director will instruct the crew to **reset**. Furniture, props and actors must go back to their original positions, or **marks**. Wardrobe and make-up will check and make sure that everything is how it should be at the beginning of the scene, e.g., if the plot requires one character to throw a glass of water over another character, then wardrobe will have to provide identical, and dry, clothes for every take. Once the director is happy with a take, the 1st A.D. will call for the crew to

move on to the next set-up. The camera will be moved, meaning that the lighting will have to be re-arranged and members of the design department will have to ensure that everything in the line of the camera's sight is how it should be. Once again, the performers will have to wait patiently until everything is ready and they are called back on set.

When the same scene is shot from many different angles – with close-ups on each of the actor's faces, as well as shots from further away – the biggest task for everyone is restoring **continuity**. Each actor has to make sure that they look the same and make the same moves and **hit their marks** at the same moment in the script, every time the scene is shot. Wardrobe and make-up will take instant photographs to check on exactly how the actor looks to ensure that nothing changes between shots. The design department and stage hands will move props, doors and pieces of furniture back to their original positions or **marks**.

It's a rule on set that actors should only touch props or move furniture during a rehearsal or a take, at all other times it is the job of the stage hands to move things.

Ex-child actress Evelyn Coull, says, 'I was 13 when I began and I don't really know how I settled into it, I guess I just followed what everyone around me was doing. I probably felt I was an adult at the time. Everyone around me was so lovely and helpful and supportive but it did make me grow up earlier than most of the other people my age. I enjoyed it so much from day one, and as I grew older and the part developed I enjoyed it even more. I never found it difficult to learn lines, it just seemed to come naturally. When I look back we worked very long hours, but for a 13 year-old it didn't feel like work, it was all so new and exciting!'

The producer who cast Evelyn in her role, Peter May, says of her, 'She was working with a very experienced crew. They were terrific in helping her learn and adapt to what was a very odd or strange environment for her. They were very supportive, but in addition to that, Evelyn was eternally curious. She wanted to know exactly what was happening. She wasn't content to just to come in and be told to stand there, and to say her lines. She wanted to know what was going on. What was the process of recording the sound? What was the lighting director doing underneath that blanket? Why were the stagehands putting tapes on the floor? She was so smart and bright that she very quickly learned that her positions were being marked, that the position of a door was being marked, so that when you shot the reverse angle of the initial shot everything would be in the same place, the actors would be in the same place, the angle of the door would be in the same place. She was very quickly spotting things that were wrong, continuity-wise. She was so interested and attentive that she just soaked it all up and was really the consummate professional almost from day one.'

Being active, not passive, helps any child on a film or television set. The crew is far more likely to support a child who is keen to learn. No one wants to have to drum things into a child who isn't interested and doesn't care. Peter May sums up the qualities that help a young actor to be successful, 'The key factors are *curiosity*, wanting to know what's going on around you, what other people's jobs are and how they relate to you; *intelligence*, being able to understand how it all works, why you need to do reverse shots, how it all cuts together in the editing suite from a series of apparently unrelated fragments of shots; and *sensitivity*, realising other people are working, and not getting in their way. Evelyn struck a lovely balance, she was always alert and curious to know what was going on but she never made a nuisance of herself.'

When a performer has finished their day's work, they will be informed that they are **wrapped**, or clear and free to leave.

The chaperone – a special look at the job
Most of the time you will assume the job of chaperone yourself. It's therefore very important that you familiarise yourself with the responsibilities.

Any child working in the public entertainment or media industry must be supervised by an adult solely responsible for the child's welfare. Whether it is in theatre, photographic work or film, on a shoot, at rehearsals and auditions, at all times whilst a child is working they must be accompanied by a chaperone.

Diana Bell, a professional chaperone, explains, 'A large percentage of these chaperones are the child's parents, but some, such as myself, work in this way as a full time career. As a freelance nursery nurse and ex-theatre manager I was always able to find work of this type, once I'd got the licence. One chaperone may take charge of up to 12 children, but may not take on any other duties.'

Parents accompanying their own children don't require a licence, but anyone wishing to become a professional chaperone has to obtain a licence, often known as a *Matron's Licence*. It is issued by the chaperone's local education authority and conditions vary from county to county. Diana continues, 'Having moved around a lot, and needing to renew the licence every year, I have experienced several different systems: at one extreme, being interviewed at home and with the authority running police checks, at the other, simply having to sign a form. Some authorities issued a photo ID card, some just handed out a photocopied licence with the last applicant's name tippexed out and mine written in.'

Looking after a baby on a shoot involves making sure that the baby is clean and comfortable. Always remember that you have the right to step in if the baby is becoming over-tired or distressed by the demands of the photographer or director. On most baby shoots, however, everyone is well used to working with babies, and they are almost always treated very well. Diana says, 'My godson, as a baby, was a model and I accompanied him to several shoots. These mainly consisted of mums and babies sitting around gossiping and was like any church hall toddler group, not a very far stretch from the normal life of a modern baby. At this stage most mothers are doing this for their own pleasure rather than to help the child's career or make money, so babies' chaperones are 99 percent mums. This trend continues through most cases of toddler and young child performers, so the main part of my chaperoning work has been with older children and teenagers.'

Theatres regularly employ chaperones to take charge of their children's choruses, particularly in professional pantomimes and musicals. Often the local children's dance school will be called upon to provide the child performers, and the dance teachers are ideal chaperones, but still need to obtain a licence.

On matinee days the chaperone may also need to supervise the children between the afternoon and evening performances, during which time they may have to escape to a place where the kids can let off steam, as well as be fed and watered and make phone calls home. A great part of the chaperone's time is spent making sure the children's make-up and costumes aren't soiled.

Touring shows involve the chaperone in travelling with the children and checking out accommodation. They are on call 24 hours a day to take care of problems such as homesickness.

Many stage schools, especially those with casting agencies attached, employ chaperones to ferry their pupils to auditions, castings and jobs. Diana confirms this, 'I've worked with a lot of teenagers from a stage school in South London, an area I didn't know at all, but this was no problem as the teenagers were auditioning in the various studios so regularly that they knew which tube to get where, the name of the receptionist and everything else, so it was more a case of me following them around!'

As most parents are already aware, teenagers can present the greatest challenge. Television director David Dunn, recalls one experience he had with a group who were put up at a hotel next to the studio, 'Do not assume that the demure uniformed child at audition – whom the stage school teacher assures you is a responsible form captain, from a loving home, who is regularly in bed by 9pm – is all that he seems, once freed from civilising restraints. Ensconced on expenses in the hotel next to the television studio, he may well be in bed by 9pm, but with whom, drinking what, and watching what on the adult channel is anyone's guess. On my programme budget I once had to pay for the restocking of a floorful of minibars and sundry other costs before realising that kids away from home do not behave like *The Famous Five*, content with a dormitory feast of ginger beer and assorted tuck. I learned not to rely on parents to inculcate a sense of responsibility into their would-be stars, and not to rely on hotel managers to take the necessary steps for you, for it's money on the bill for them.'

Such instances are very rare. Chaperone, Diana Bell says, 'One major advantage of chaperoning is that the children are usually impeccably behaved. Once over a certain age, they are there because they want to be, and know that any trouble caused or lack of good behaviour may mean them losing their job. The children knew that the punishment for any misdemeanour would mean having to sit in the wings and not take part in the next performance of the show – an intolerable prospect. Generally, performing children are confident and sociable creatures, well used to making friends and being pleasant to everyone they come across. The children rarely make the job difficult.'

Sometimes the challenge is presented by the sheer volume of a project. The scale of the Harry Potter films means setting up a whole new 'world' for the child performers. Diana explains, 'I worked on the second Harry Potter film which used over 800 children from schools all around the country, 1 chaperone per 12 children, plus a schoolroom and teacher for every 12 children. A fleet of dozens of coaches with 3 chaperones and 36 kids on each left the stage school at 7am each morning to take them to the studio.'

The chaperone's job is very demanding, involving long hours. Diana describes her working day, 'My day involved starting at 5am to get to the school for 6.30am to count kids and get them on the coach. The day at the studio was spent trying to pick out my 12 teenagers and ferry them from coach to make-up, to costume, to set, to toilet, to canteen, to schoolroom, and back, plus interminable hours sitting with the other dozens of chaperones at the edge of the set. We had to sit **off camera**, and totally silent, checking off each child's chart, the number of quarter-hours spent in each place, and silently voting on who was going to tell the director that the kids were due a break (at thousands of pounds cost to the budget). When the day's shoot was over, I had to supervise the kids on the coach, arriving back at the stage school at 7pm. I then had to wait on the pavement for parents held up in traffic, to collect their offspring. I usually finished at about 8.30pm and got home at 10pm. I was only paid for working hours with no travel expenses. I lived right by the studio but had to go to the stage school and back to accompany the children!'

It is the chaperone's job to make sure the child gets the proper breaks, to arrange for toilets and refreshments, and to ensure that education has been organised.

Diana sums up the qualities required in a chaperone, 'As long as you know how to deal with homesickness, broken friendships, teenage angst; how to spot and discreetly remove a child needing a pee amid a crowd scene; a thousand ways to silently entertain a crowd; and how to organise a trip for 13 to McDonalds in a town you don't know with a half hour time-frame, you'll have no problem. But you also need to deal with directors, stage door keepers, floor managers, adult performers, and parents. You need a real air of authority and an inside knowledge of the industry certainly helps. You also need to accept that the job, particularly on a long running stage or film production, can involve many incredibly tedious hours.'

People and their jobs

Client: The company (advertising agency, store, publication or production company) which is commissioning the shoot for an advertisement, commercial, catalogue or drama.

Photographer: The photographer is responsible for taking the photographs. They will be hired for their unique ability to compose and deliver the images a client wants. Photographers who work with children need a special talent and temperament to get the best out of children. Daniel Pangbourne gained wide experience of different types of photography, including advertising, fashion and corporate, when he was starting out as a professional photographer, but he discovered that photographing children was something he had a gift for and particularly enjoyed. He says, 'A friend offered me a kids' shoot for the cover of a catalogue. I spent a day shooting it – and I literally walked out that day and thought "That's it – found it!"'

Photographer's Assistant: May be anything from a receptionist to a baby wrangler, to trainee photographer, or any combination thereof.

Stylist: The stylist sorts out the child's clothes and the way they look, ready for the shoot. They are usually more integrated with the child than anybody.

They will normally be present at the casting when the child is chosen for the shoot, and will have been briefed on the clothes and the look which the client wants. They will take notes on the size of the child and will select all the clothes to fit and specifically to suit that child's colouring.

Baby Wrangler: A baby wrangler is responsible for coaxing babies and children to produce the performance which the photographer or television or film director, is looking for on set. Cat Sulley says, 'Every baby's different. It's all in the eye contact, getting to know the baby, getting to understand the baby. If you don't know, or don't like children, they won't like you, and you couldn't do my job. It's just one of those abilities that I discovered I had. I was working as a photographer's assistant, and people suddenly said, "Hey you can do this!" and I said, "Can't everybody?" and they said, "No!" When I work with the photographer, usually we work directly with the children without the mums. I would never take baby away, if baby wasn't happy. It's only when the baby's happy it's all right. I may say to mum, "Just stay within earshot, and if I call your name you can come in and give baby a hug." Although they call it "baby wrangler," I work with kids up to 11 years old. A lot of the time parents want to take me home!'.

Drama Coach: On movies, a drama coach will be employed to give personal attention to the children. Often in films, the director is more concerned with the pictures he is shooting: expecting actors to turn up on set with their own interpretations of the part they are playing. Children obviously require guidance, therefore a drama coach is there to devote time to them, helping them as they learn their lines and coaxing the right interpretation out of them. They will also be around the child on the set, supporting them through the many takes and repetitions of a scene, making sure that they don't tire, lose energy or let their focus slip.

Producer: The person in television or film with overall responsibility for the show and the budget, and for hiring and firing. Not always around for filming or recording, but if the producer does pay a visit, everyone will be tense and anxious to be seen to be doing their job well. This is *not* the person to ask to direct you to the toilet!

Director: The director is responsible for turning the written word into the film or TV episode which the audience will finally watch. The director interprets the script, shapes the actor's performances, decides on the the shots and the number of takes, and finally puts together the giant jigsaw puzzle of the entire drama. You may already have met the director and P.A. if there were auditions for the role, but when the production is underway, the director's focus is always entirely on the scene which is being shot at that moment – therefore it is not advisable to approach or distract the director. When it comes to your scene, the director will ask for, and expect, a specific performance and moves, and it is your child's job to deliver that. Debates or disagreements with the director on set are to be avoided at all costs.

Production Assistant (P.A.): The production assistant works at the director's side during the whole production process from beginning to end, attending rehearsals, shooting, and editing. The P.A. is responsible for keeping track of all aspects of the script, noting any changes, the number and quality of takes, and everything concerning script continuity. The P.A. deals with everything the director requires and liaises on the director's behalf with all the other members of the crew.

Researcher: On live television magazine programmes or current affairs programmes, a researcher is the person assigned to develop an idea for the show. They will be the first point of contact in setting up an appearance, and will make all the arrangements beforehand. They normally work from offices and are not involved in anything on set. On the production day they will hand over to the stage manager who will look after things in and around the studio.

1st Assistant Director (1st A.D.) (Film)**/Floor Manager (F.M.)** (TV): You can regard this person effectively as the 'Boss' of a film or television crew. They are in charge of everything and responsible for making sure that productions keep to their schedules and budgets. They run the **location**, or the **floor** and are in complete charge.

2nd Assistant Director (2nd A.D.) (Film)**/Assistant Floor Manager (A.F.M.)** (TV): Second in command to the 1st or F.M., will take care of administrative work involving locations etc.

3rd Assistant Director (3rd A.D.) (Film)**/Stage Manager (S.M.)** (TV): Responsible for making sure that cast and extras get on set on time. Will produce call sheets and get the information you need to you. Depending on the size of the shoot, will be your main point of contact on a shoot. Large shoots may have **4th Assistant Director (4th A.D.)** (Film)**/Assistant Stage manager (A.S.M.)** (TV) to assist them.

Make-up Department: Responsible for hair and make-up of all models or performers. Also responsible for continuity. They will take instant photographs and will look after make-up and hair throughout the shoot.

Wardrobe Department: Responsible for clothes of all models or performers. Also responsible for continuity. They will take instant photographs and will look after clothes throughout the shoot.

Camera Operator: Operates the camera and composes the shots to suit the director's requirements.

Lighting Director: In charge of the lighting on location or in studio.

Gaffer: In charge of everything electrical, including the supply of electricity by generator, on location. Looks after cables and safety.

Sound Recordist: In charge of sound. Makes sure everyone is covered by microphones and checks sound levels and balance as it is being recorded.

Boom Operator: Holds and points the microphone which is held on a long pole, called the **boom**.

Design Department: Responsible for the design. In other words, the 'look' of every studio and exterior location. They will design and build rooms to fit inside studios and furnish them appropriately. They will transform an exterior location, like a street, to fit Victorian times. They are responsible for everything from disguising electricity pylons in period dramas, to creating small props, like providing a passport or other official document for a character in a story.

Catering: Provides all the food and drink for crew and cast on location.

Stage Hand: Assists in moving props or anything else around a set.

Grips: Lay tracks and cable for the camera to run along on a **dolly**.

Runner: A general helper, who might be asked to assist anyone on a set.

Terminology

Layout: The plan for a photographic shoot.

Script: The story, dialogue and action for a film, TV drama, or commercial.

Location: Any real place – in the countryside or town, out of doors or inside, a street, a park, an office, a house – which is being used to represent a place in the drama being filmed. It may be altered by the design department to represent another place, or it may simply be used as it is.

Studio: The entire area in a television centre including the control rooms and the part where a drama is being recorded.

Studio floor: or simply **Floor** Refers to the large, sealed-off area which houses the cameras and sets like theatre sets, constructed and dressed by designers to fit the drama.

Set: The part of a location or studio which the cameras will be shooting. If someone is 'on set', or if you are asked to go 'on set' that means the area in front of the cameras, where the drama is actually being filmed. It refers only to the part in front of the cameras.

Control room: This is where directors, P.A.s and vision mixers and sound technicians work in a television drama. Director, P.A. and vision mixer will be in one control room, with the sound technicians in another control room.

NB: Remember that everyone in a studio is connected by microphones, speakers and headsets. The people in the control rooms can hear everything which is being said on the studio floor, and all the members of the crew can hear each other and everyone in the control room through their headsets. Every word uttered has the possibility of being picked up by a microphone and broadcast through loudspeakers in the control room, so don't get caught saying anything about anyone which you wouldn't say to their face!

Green room: The place where the actors sit and wait to be called to perform. Normally with refreshments, water, tea, coffee etc.

Named/featured part: A leading role in a drama, or a major role with a named character, requiring direction and featuring in one or more scenes.

Extra: A background role in a drama, non-speaking.

Walk-on: A background role in a drama, but one where some specific action is required perhaps with a line to speak (more money is paid for this).

Schedule: The timetable for a project from beginning to end.

Call: The order to be somewhere, such as at the studio, on location, at wardrobe or make-up etc. You might be asked to wait to 'be called' or to be given your 'call'.

Call Sheet: The timetable which tells you when and where all the various 'calls' are.

Call time: The time you are expected to be at any particular place, e.g. on set or at wardrobe or make-up.

Shoot: The job of recording, filming, or photographing, on location or in studio.

Scene: A script is divided into scenes, each scene moves the story forward and its action takes place at a single location or at single point in time.

Shot: When a camera is recording or filming, or a photograph is being taken.

Take: A piece of action, a scene or merely a small part of a scene, which is recorded or filmed in a single continuous shot without a break.

Set-up: The way a set or location looks for a particular take.

On Camera or **On Set:** The area in front – within range – of the cameras on location or in a studio.

Off Camera or **Off Set:** The area behind – out of range – of the cameras on location or in a studio.

Stand By or **Standing By:** The instruction to be in state of readiness, being ready to go.

Rolling: When the camera operator starts shooting.

Filming and **Recording:** Basically the same action of recording images. Filming, however, refers only to film – which has to be processed and developed before it can be viewed – while recording refers to video, either on tape or disk, an instant process which allows the material to be played back immediately.

On-air: In a television studio, this signifies that the cameras are live or that the tapes are running, i.e., the programme in studio is either being recorded or is being transmitted live.

Walk-through: When the director will ask the actors to go through their movements during a scene, to allow the camera and sound departments to accommodate their moves.

Rehearsal: To practise a scene without recording for the benefit of all parties.

Action: The instruction to everyone that the take to be recorded is about to start.

Cut: The instruction to everyone that the take being recorded has come to an end.

Moving On or **Move On:** The instruction that a scene or take has been successfully completed and that cast and crew are ready to go on to the next thing on the schedule.

Wrap: The instruction that work is over for the day. It can be applied to an actor who has finished work and is not required for the rest of that day.

Reset: To go back to the beginning of the take. And to put everything (including the actors) back to their original marks.

Props: Properties are anything on a set, from furniture to bottles and glasses.

Mark: The spots on a set marking the starting position and finishing position of anything which moves during a take: an actor, a door, a prop.

POV: Point of View. In other words, the camera is placed to see things as the actor would see them, and so that is what the audience will see (commonly used in horror films, where we have the **POV** of the murderer so that we don't see the murderer's face, we only see their prey).

Reverse: When two actors are having a conversation in a scene, there will often be a close-up of one actor's face, intercut with a close-up of the other actor's face. The second shot here is known as a **reverse** or **reverse angle**.

Close-up: When the camera is up close on an actor's face

Mid Shot: When the camera is taking in the top half of the actor's body.

Long Shot: When the camera is taking in the whole of an actor's body.

2 (or more) Shot: When the camera is taking in 2 (or more) actors involved in a scene.

Dolly: A construction on wheels which runs on tracks. It holds the camera and a seat for the camera operator. It allows the camera to move smoothly across an area on location, letting the camera follow actors as they walk, for example.

Cherry Picker: A lift which allows the camera and its operator to rise up and take shots from above, or to start from a high point and swoop down.

Boom: The long pole with a microphone at one end which is kept out of range of the cameras and directed towards the actors above their heads as they speak.

Continuity: One of the most important aspects of drama production. Every time the crew and cast stop and start recording or filming, everything has to match precisely so that the jigsaw of shots and scenes fit together. Each department (wardrobe, make-up, design, actors etc.) must make sure that when they are asked to repeat a scene, everything is repeated precisely. Also remember that one scene might follow another in the story, but it may be recorded *beforehand*, or the two scenes might be recorded weeks apart. For this reason, all the departments keep accurate records (by using instant photographs). For example, if it is raining in one scene, and the actors end the scene by entering a house, then when the scene inside the house is recorded, the wardrobe department will have to make sure that they make the actor's clothes wet.

CHAPTER SEVEN CHECKLIST

Ten facts to find out from your agent as soon as you are told about the job:
1. Name of company.
2. Name of contact person.
3. Description of your child's job.
4. What wardrobe and props are required.
5. What are the make-up and hair requirements.
6. Address of location.
7. What transportation is being provided.
8. The dates and times you are required.
9. What refreshments will be provided.
10. What the fee is.

Questions to ask when you arrive at a job:
1. Ask for the names of key personnel.
   On a photographic shoot: the photographer, photographer's assistant, the stylist, the baby wrangler.
   On a TV or film shoot: the director, the A.D. (assistant director, floor manager), the P.A. (production assistant), wardrobe, make-up.
2. Ask where the toilet facilities are.
3. Ask what the refreshment facilities are.
4. Ask when you'll be required to start work.
5. Ask where you should wait when you aren't required.

Twenty points to remember when working on a shoot:
1. Professional behaviour is expected at all times.
2. One child, one chaperone is the rule.
3. Know your child's rights.
4. Know your child's place.
5. Keep quiet on set.
6. Be prepared for boredom and take things along to keep your child occupied.
7. Be careful about what your child eats on working days.
8. Don't take food or drink on to the set.
9. Pay attention to instructions.
10. Don't touch or remove anything from the set.
11. Never change your child's clothes, hair or make-up.
12. If you take a break, tell someone where you are going.
13. Take a favourite toy for your baby.
14. Don't carry valuables with you.

CHAPTER SEVEN CHECKLIST (CONT.)

15. If you are doing background or extra work, keep a low profile and make sure you eat at the correct catering table or counter.
16. If there are any problems or disputes on set, be calm and discreet when dealing with them. Refer to your agent if necessary.
17. Don't forget anything.
18. Check out. Ensure you are clear to leave, and confirm the number of hours you have worked.
19. Confidentiality. Remember that you have privileged information. Keep the details of all work confidential.
20. Finally ... report back to your agent with details of the hours that you have worked, and tell your agent if there have been any problems.

Fifteen things to remember when packing a bag for work:
1. All the information (in plastic pockets) which you need about the shoot.
2. Spare plastic pockets for receipts.
3. Paper and pen for taking notes.
4. Clean underwear or changing kit for baby (with sufficient changes for the day).
5. Baby wipes.
6. Tissues.
7. Sun protection cream (with a high protection factor) if working outdoors.
8. Simple change of clothes in case of spills.
9. Books, paper and pencils, activity pack or favourite toy for baby.
10. Make-up cover stick for any blemishes.
11. Hairbrush, comb, clasps or hairbands.
12. Healthy snacks or drinks (without sugar).
13. Repair kit: safety pins, needle and thread.
14. First aid kit: antiseptic wipes and sticking plasters in case of scrapes.
15. Any medications your child might require.

CHAPTER EIGHT
A Star is Born
What happens next?

The working child

Now that your child is working you have a new set of responsibilities and concerns. In every person's life there is no period of greater change than the first 16 years. No matter how talented your youngster is, they will find themselves falling victim to the side effects of growing up.

Babies and toddlers can quickly establish themselves as stars with advertisers. They may get a lot of work, and as they reach the age of five or six, having been in the business for a few years, will be becoming accustomed to their celebrity status. It's not unusual for children so young to decide that they want to pursue a career in performance.

Then ... their teeth fall out. Suddenly no one wants them. The six to eight year-old age group suffers terribly from this. Clients will often specify 'Must have perfect teeth'. Even when new teeth grow in, often they are disproportionately large and the change this makes to the child's face means that they have lost the cute look that they had during their early years; so the child finds that still no one wants to work with them.

Those children who survive their 'teething troubles' can be affected from the age of 11 onwards when puberty gets underway and their hormones start to go haywire. The physical changes at this age can transform a girl into the presage of a beautiful young woman, or turn an engaging boy into an awkward, acne-covered youth! These are difficult times for any parent, but combine this with the career path of a child model and you have a potential emotional minefield. It's up to the parent and the agent to support the child through it all and to protect them from other perceived dangers.

The potential hazards
Losing out on childhood
Some people feel that there is a danger of a loss of innocence for any child working with adults, though most of the people who have experience of this agree that it gives a child an added advantage.

Former child actress, Evelyn Coull, says, 'I don't feel that I missed out on childhood in any way at all. It prepared me well for what working life was going to be like and made me a lot more confident and comfortable in an adult working environment.'

Brother and sister, David and Rachel York, both successful child models and actors, now grown-up, agree. David says, 'It made me realise that I could talk to adults on their level, and it made me much more confident about what I wanted to do with my life.' Rachel concurs, 'Going to castings and jobs, you gain a lot of confidence. But you are *absolutely* allowed to be a kid, after all that's *why* you're there ... to be a child. I'd never say you lose out on your childhood.'

Remember to balance work and play. It will be up to you, the parent, to ensure that your child doesn't miss out on the things that other children their age are enjoying.

Losing touch with normality and reality
There would seem to be evidence – especially in Hollywood – that fame and fortune can have fatal consequences for children. The well-publicised cases of drink or drug addiction, premature deaths, and even suicides of former child stars can cause people to assert that being young, rich and famous will inevitably lead to disaster. But there are many hundreds of children who have worked and earned large amounts of money from modelling and acting, and whose lives haven't come to a tragic end.

Agent, Janis Penn, observes, 'If a child is going to go off the rails, they're going to do it anyway. Modelling and acting are just activities like football or swimming or netball or judo. It's a great experience for them and the confidence it builds might be good for them in other aspects of their lives. Scare stories are just that. There is a lot of legislation to protect children and their parents or chaperones are around to look after them every minute.'

Actor and singer, Aidan Bell, agrees, 'As in all walks of life there are both good and bad apples in the barrel. Occasionally a child performer will suffer badly – famously Lena Zavaroni – but in general terms, for every Zavaroni there must be thousands and thousands of kids who don't "make it" and for whom being involved in modelling is not exploitation, nor does it adversely affect them in any way, rather it is fun and encourages their self worth and social skills.'

Becoming arrogant, precocious or egotistical

The more successful a child is, the more difficult it will be for them to keep a healthy perspective on their self-importance. David York says, 'You can't help but be proud about what you're doing. I'd get videos of work that I had been doing and I'd show them to my friends. I wouldn't talk about the money side of it to them, though. Because I knew people don't like to have that sort of thing pushed on them. But I know there are some kids out there that are doing that. There are some kids who'll love to show off about the whole thing, money and all ... "Look at me, I'm special!" Those are the kids you have to worry about, because the other kids are going to think, "Okay. I don't like this one," and they could find themselves in trouble.'

Parents are the ones who must look out for and moderate this behaviour. Donna Hearn, mother of model daughters, says, 'Becky and Charlie aren't precocious at all about it. They don't think of the fact that they're modelling, it's just something they do. It's the most natural thing in the world to them. I try to keep their feet on the ground, I don't like horrible children that are full of themselves!'

Aidan Bell believes personality traits are part of a person's nature, 'I feel that people, whether children or adults, do not change so much. I believe that both a bubbly, happy personality or a gruff, moody one will remain so whether prince or pauper.'

If your child does start to display characteristics that you don't like, it might be difficult trying to talk them into changing their behaviour. David

York says, 'One thing, above all, I've learned about working with kids, and having been a kid myself, is that they never, ever, take your advice! You can say, "Don't be too open about this or that," and "Don't be too brash" and "Don't go on about what you're doing too much." But if they want to do it – they'll do it. They have to learn the hard way. Maybe it'll come when they get a black eye from some other kid who gets fed up listening when they take it too far ... "Okay, yeh, yeh, shut up now" and ... Thwack! That'll get the message across to them more than logic!'

Work interfering with school

It is claimed that working can interfere with a child's education, but education is an area which is tightly regulated. Children working on long contracts for films must have a tutor provided and as agent Janis Penn points out for the rest, 'They're only allowed to work ten days out of every six months. It can't take over their lives.'

Former child actress, Evelyn Coull, has strong opinions about her time working in television, 'It never affected my schoolwork at all. I went on to study at Glasgow University. I worked as a television presenter all the way through university and during the summer months presented a radio programme up in Stornoway. At the end of my course, I graduated with a 2:1 honours degree!'

Mother of model daughters, Donna Hearn, doesn't feel that her girls' school work, or their ambitions, have been affected by their work. She says, 'Becky's got the potential to act – but she says she wants to be a teacher because they get lots of holidays. Charlie wants to be a lawyer. Neither of them have ever said they'd like to carry on doing it. They're both very clever girls, but if modelling has done anything, it has given them a lot of confidence.'

Obsession with body image, leading to eating disorders

There is no doubt that girls – and boys, too – from all walks of life can fall prey to eating disorders such as anorexia nervosa. The influence of images projected by the media are often held responsible. There are accounts of dancers – particularly ballet dancers – and catwalk models feeling under pressure to cut down on their eating until it becomes an obsession which takes over their lives. There is no evidence that acting can lead to this, though Evelyn Coull admits, 'I hated watching myself on screen. I had some very dodgy hairstyles and even worse clothes. I remember being very critical of myself.' But she didn't let it affect her, 'Eventually I just got used to it,' she says.

Rachel York, now working in an agency, says, 'I've never encountered anorexia in the agency. Perhaps it's more in catwalk and fashion modelling. In commercials or drama, people are cast because they look the part. We need all shapes and sizes.'

Agent, Janis Penn, says, 'I can only remember one occasion when we had that sort of experience, and as far as I could see the mother was responsible! She kept talking about her daughter's arms being flabby looking. We *never* ask children to diet. Never. Our clients are looking for *real* kids. *Real* people. And they're looking for all shapes and sizes. All characters. All types. We often get asked for children who are overweight! So we're looking for a good selection. We were recently asked to cast a refugee family, obviously then we were looking for skinny children. And so yes, we have naturally thin kids on our books, but by no means are they the ones who get all the work!'

The benefits
Earning money which can be laid aside for the future
Former child model and actor, David York, now working in a model agency says, 'I was making quite a lot of money as a child. What my friends would earn in a year from doing a paper round, I could make in a week! One of the biggest jobs I did was for a car commercial in the United States, and for a week's work I made a huge sum. Right now we've got one kid in a commercial. He appears for a second and he's going to get £25,000 – more than some *adults* get for working for a year. Even as a kid you know it's easy money. My mum thought it was very important to keep my feet on the ground, so the money that I earned from my jobs helped to pay for school fees. My parents left it up to me, but they did convince me that it was best to be investing in

the future – investing in my life. I had no objection to contributing. I had a good childhood. I wasn't spoiled. My parents didn't want me to be spoiled. That's not to say they wouldn't allow me to have squandered the money that I was earning. But if a child does become successful, and the money is put aside for them until they're older, it could buy them a car, or pay the deposit on a house. You've got something there. You've got something to give you start in life. And if you can control yourself, or if your parents can convince you to, then you've got a real advantage.'

David's sister Rachel, agrees, 'If I had a kid who was making a lot of money, I would lock it up, put it in a trust fund, never let him know what he had earned. Then when he was 18 or 21, I could say, "Well, that's your deposit for your flat. Well done!" But we do see mothers who let their children squander their money. I bet when these kids grow up they'll look back and think of all the things they could have done with it. I think it's down to the parents. When I was working, I didn't even know there was money involved! I was doing it for fun. At the end of the day, the money goes into the child's account. In their name. But the parent has control when they're young. When I turned 16 I wanted to go on holiday and my mum said, "Well, you've got this money from modelling ..." And I was so pleased, I took it and went on holiday. But even now, I look back and regret that I spent that money on a holiday!'

Donna Hearn, speaks about how she handles her daughters' earnings, 'When their money comes in to the bank I always give them a little treat. I let them go out and buy something, nothing very expensive, but what they want, they can have. I like them to know they're getting rewarded for what they're doing. But the rest of the money, I put away for them. They've each got a nest egg they'll get at about 18. I want to make sure they don't squander it. It's a substantial amount each that they have. It will make a difference to their lives. A car. A deposit for a house.'

Lesley Simpson is also concerned that her daughter doesn't squander the money, 'Tiffany has children's bonds put aside to mature for her when she's 18 and 21.'

A step up the ladder to a successful career

Former child actress, Evelyn Coull, feels that being introduced to working in television as a child has ended up shaping her career, 'Since "Machair" I have been involved in media. That's where I am working now, I got a job two months ago as a radio producer and I'm really enjoying it. I have missed acting a lot and would love to do some more. But I have gained so much experience, both in television and radio through my years at university that I am very lucky to be in the position that I am. Ideally I would really like to do some more presenting and acting. I'd like to go on to do some writing and am working on radio ideas at the moment. I'm also planning to write a book. Acting was what brought me to the media. It's very hard to say whether I would have been enticed in another way if it wasn't for that ... who knows!'

Lesley Simpson's daughter has also been influenced by her work, 'Tiffany wants to be a professional dancer. She goes to classes every week. In one of her classes the other members are in the 14 – 21 age group, and she's at their level, but too young to take the exams! So being in this business all helps. It's what she wants to do. Also, Tiffany earns her own money. She pays for her own dancing lessons. She's very well-balanced.'

Maturity and confidence

Working in an adult environment helps children to be at ease in adult situations, but that doesn't necessarily make them precocious. Journalist Gavin Docherty, who has interviewed many 'child stars' says, 'I really enjoyed interviewing the kids – I found they had no pretensions. They were willing talkers, natural, honest, no phoniness or fakery. They're great so long as you don't talk down to them ... don't treat them like kids. Some of the big stars could learn a thing or two from them.'

David York says, 'The adults around you treat you like their equal. It's all, "Hey, how are you doing? Are you all right? Can I get you anything?" They're friends with you. So you react to them and behave with them in a different way. It makes you treat people differently. It's not arrogance. I don't think I ever became arrogant. I just realised that the people around me were like bigger versions of kids ... who talk in deeper voices and have slightly more wrinkles. So that was good.'

The parent's role
Looking after the finances
Agent, Janis Penn explains, 'Parents are entitled to take a certain amount from the child's money. It varies from authority to authority. Some will say you can only deduct expenses. Some will say 30 percent, some say 50 percent. The child is entitled to spend the money – it doesn't have to go into a trust fund.' But she reminds parents that children also have a tax liability, 'Children get the same personal allowance as an adult. Then expenses come off. Then they have to pay tax.'

Book Keeping
Your child is now a self-employed model or actor. Whether or not their earnings amount to enough to pay tax, you should be accounting for all the money that comes in and goes out in the course of their 'business'. It need only be a simple record of income and expenditure.

Write on the back of all the receipts, or staple a note to each saying exactly what it was for. Do this as soon as possible. You may think you'll remember later, but inevitably memories fade. Store the receipts safely in plastic pockets in your folder. As mentioned earlier, a ring binder with plastic pocket files is a good way to keep the details of each job together, and track the progress.

You should always keep a record of each job so that you can follow it from beginning to end. Follow each job through the following steps:

The Casting:
Note the job and the location of the casting.
Keep receipts for any expenses:
- travelling expenses, petrol, train, taxi or bus fares
- lunch or snacks while you were away from home
- any clothes you had to buy for your child for the casting

If your child is cast, follow through to ...

The Job:

Note the job dates and the name of the job and contact.

Note the hours that you worked (and of course, make sure your agent knows).

Note the fee which is due.

Note when you receive the fee.

If you divide the money (into savings plans or trust funds) keep notes about where it all goes.

Keep receipts for any expenses:

■ travelling expenses, petrol, train, taxi or bus fares
■ lunch or snacks while you were away from home
■ any clothes you had to buy for your child for the job

Note all other expenses:

■ photographs
■ agency fees
■ telephone calls
■ stationery etc.

All expenses can be offset against taxes if your child earns enough to be liable for tax.

At the end of each year, go through your folder, and make a two lists. The first should be all the earnings, or income from your child's modelling; the second, your expenditure, all the money you spent on anything involved with your child's modelling. Subtract the total expenditure from the total income, and you should be left with the amount of profit.

If your child begins to earn large sums of money it is best to get the advice of an accountant. However, do remember that an accountant will still require all your receipts – so it is imperative that you *keep everything safe*.

Coping with working, success and failure

While your child is working, you will be responsible for looking after their rights and well-being. You will also be responsible for keeping your child's feet on the ground and taking care of their earnings. Another challenge will come when your child has to deal with not being in the spotlight any more.

Sometimes a child who has been working a lot suddenly announces that they don't want to do it anymore. They move on to secondary school and boys might want to play more football, while girls become self-conscious about puberty.

But inevitably some children will face rejection and have to come to terms with it. Donna Hearn relates an experience which demonstrates how fickle the world of modelling and acting can be, 'Charlie was the main child in a commercial and there was a possibility that the whole family would appear. They picked us all up in a car to take us to Brighton for the shoot, while everybody else arrived in a coach. But when they gave Charlie the clothes to put on, she hated them and let them know it. So they took the clothes and offered them to another little girl, who was immediately given the main part!' Donna's family were still used as extras but Donna describes how the treatment they received changed, 'As soon as Charlie was no longer the main child, we were asked to get our stuff out of the car and told to get the coach back with everyone else. When you're the star – they can't do enough for you but when you're just an extra it's another story!'

Keeping other interests alive and active

Adapting to a change in fortune can be difficult for a successful child. One of the best ways to handle it is to have other interests to turn to. Changing focus to something else which your child enjoys, and which they are good at, will help to take the sting out of any feelings of rejection if their modelling or acting career comes to an end.

Looking to the future ...

Some children never stop working and go on to become adult actors. Some children use the skills they have learned to go on to find other careers, still related to the business. But for some, a modelling career is just a small part of their childhood, leaving them with superb experiences, memories, tapes, photographs and perhaps a substantial nest egg in the bank.

One final reminder ...

You might be thinking now that there is much more to the business than you ever imagined. It may seem daunting. Perhaps now is the right time for one final reminder from agent Janis Penn, 'Children love it! And it's not hard work for them. They can do it. And a lot of them even surprise their own parents. A lot of the parents come back to us and they say, "I can't believe Little Johnny worked so well, he brought tears to my eyes, he was great ... terrific!" We hear this all the time. It's lovely.'

It can be great fun, and great experience, but never forget that your child is doing a professional job in a professional environment. And you have a job, too. So you both have to consider yourselves as professionals. The more professional you are the more easily you will fit in, and the more smoothly things will run

OTHER USEFUL SOURCES OF INFORMATION

The Stage
A publication featuring news, reviews and features about every aspect of the arts and entertainment industry.
Available (usually by ordering) from newsagents; with an online version at:
http://www.thestage.co.uk

Spotlight
Directories of actors, actresses, presenters, drama school graduates, stunt artists, children and young performers. These volumes are used by casting professionals. The website address is:
http://www.spotlightcd.com/index.html

British Arts
An online directory of Arts including the Performing Arts in the UK.
http://www.britisharts.co.uk

Conference of Drama Schools
The representative body for the leading drama schools in the UK.
Enquiries to:
Executive Secretary
CDS
PO Box 34252
London
NW5 1XJ
Their useful and comprehensive website can be found at
http://www.drama.ac.uk

INDEX